*— EXTINGUISHING ANXIETY & **IGNITING HOPE** —*

FIREPROOF
Happiness

— *EXTINGUISHING ANXIETY & IGNITING HOPE* —

FIREPROOF
Happiness

DR. RANDY ROSS

Published by Best Seller Publishing®, St. Augustine, FL
Best Seller Publishing® is a registered trademark
Printed in the United States of America.
ISBN: 978-1-956649-78-9

This publication is designed to provide accurate and authoritative information with regard to the subject matter covered. It is sold with the understanding that the publisher is not engaged in rendering legal, accounting, or other professional advice. If legal advice or other expert assistance is required, the services of a competent professional should be sought. The opinions expressed by the authors in this book are not endorsed by Best Seller Publishing® and are the sole responsibility of the author rendering the opinion.

For more information, please write:
Best Seller Publishing®
53 Marine Street
St. Augustine, FL 32084
or call 1(626) 765 9750

Visit us online at: www.BestSellerPublishing.org

— IN PRAISE OF —
FIREPROOF
Happiness

"*Fireproof Happiness* is the right book at the right time. During these taxing times, so many of us can enrich our own lives and those around us with a little (or a lot) more hope and inspiration."

"Hope is a powerful force for good for those who understand it and know how to embrace it. In *Fireproof Happiness*, Dr. Randy Ross both explains the impact of hope and provides practical ways to put hope into practice, impacting your life and your leadership. Hope is the best strategy if you want to garner significant results."

"Hope is the fuel that propels individuals, teams and organizations forward through tumultuous times. If you are looking for a message that will energize you to persevere and perform at a higher level, while preparing you to lead others through difficulties, then *Fireproof Happiness* will help you do just that."

"Hope is a powerful force for good. It lays the foundation for all great strategy, fuels engagement and imbues teams with the confidence they need to accomplish the extraordinary. The message of *Fireproof Happiness* provides both principles and practices that will allow anyone to embrace and face life's most challenging issues."

RICK GRAF, PRESIDENT & CEO, PINNACLE & NATIONAL APARTMENT ASSOCIATION, CHAIRMAN OF THE BOARD, 2021

"Hope isn't just *nice to have*, it's vital to possess in challenging times and necessary if you want to soar in life and leadership. Dr. Randy brings this point home simply and clearly in a message that has the power to change your perspective and your life. Embrace the message of *Fireproof Happiness* and it will change you for the better."

JAY GEIER, FOUNDER & CEO, SCHEDULING INSTITUTE

"Looking at life and daily decisions through a hope-filled lens is critical to our emotional health and well-being. In *Fireproof Happiness*, Dr. Ross provides a recipe for a happy life. A great read for all, especially during times when curveballs are becoming more common each day."

JIMMY TAYLOR, VICE PRESIDENT, OPERATIONS, IHG (INTERCONTINENTAL HOTEL GROUP)

"Dr. Randy Ross has done it again! Specializing in taking a common concept we all need, he explores hope in such a way as to provide uncommon insights that yield a profound impact. If you want a methodology to build a better tomorrow, you don't have to hope to find it. You just did!"

DAVID SALYERS, VICE PRESIDENT, MARKETING, CHICK-FIL-A (RETIRED)

"For anyone who knows Randy, they know this conversation about hope is authentic to his core. As our world experiences the failure of so many of the social and economic systems we've relied on for centuries, developing an understanding of and building a foundation on hope couldn't be more relevant or important."

DAVID PYLE, SENIOR VICE PRESIDENT,
ENTERPRISE PARTNERSHIPS, COX AUTOMOTIVE INC.

"Dr. Ross' message of hope is highly relevant and timely. We are at a turning point in business and in life. The new normal isn't normal at all. Many employees are worried, frightened, confused and need new levels of leadership. A leadership style that has its foundations built on the power of hope and optimism is a game-changer for business recovery, high-performance team development and building an amazing company culture."

STEPHEN CHILDS, GTML™, CHIEF HUMAN RESOURCE OFFICER,
PANASONIC AUTOMOTIVE

"In *Fireproof Happiness*, Dr. Randy Ross provides direly needed guidance in times of disruption and life-altering challenges. Built upon the cornerstone that 'acceptance of reality is the defining characteristic of hope,' Randy shares a compelling model of hope that is engaging, empowering and motivating – leading to practical steps we each can take."

PAUL WHITE, PH.D, CO-AUTHOR OF THE BEST-SELLER
THE 5 LANGUAGES OF APPRECIATION IN THE WORKPLACE

"There may never be a more appropriate time for this book. *Fireproof Happiness* is exactly the message needed for these uncertain times. Dr. Ross has a unique ability to communicate in a way that resonates with his readers. His message of being your authentic self and focusing on hope to create the future you want is spot on. This book is a must read, whether for business or personal development. Hope is the strategy for Love, Life and Business. Bravo!"

SHAWN HANDRAHAN, PRESIDENT & CEO, VALET LIVING

"Too many leaders see hope as soft or magical and, therefore, an excuse to procrastinate. Dr. Ross shows us that hope is a force-multiplier in our lives and leadership."

RON KITCHENS, AUTHOR OF *UNIQUELY YOU*

"In unprecedented times, you need unprecedented guidance. Dr. Randy Ross provides exactly that in this easy to read playbook on the impact hope has on our everyday lives. I have heard my whole career that hope wasn't a strategy, but it didn't sit well with what I knew to be true in my heart. Backed by scientific research and accompanied with practical applications, Dr. Ross shows that hope is, indeed, the best strategy! Elevate yourself and your teams with hope."

STEVE BLACK, CEO & FOUNDER, A BRIGHTER DAY

"A mushrooming number of people are seeking strength and direction in these tumultuous times. Dr. Randy Ross delivers fresh, well-researched insight and engaging principles that will impact your life for the good. The great tragedy in life is that too many people settle for second or even third best and, in so doing, never discover the best in life. *Fireproof Happiness* serves up an antidote to treat our tendency to settle, and challenges us to rise up to be our very best by harnessing hope."

DOUG DEAN, CHIEF HUMAN RESOURCE OFFICER, CHILDREN OF ALABAMA

To my children: Ryan, Lindsay, Colton and Jonathan.
May these principles give you the guidance
and direction to create a better tomorrow,
as you build your futures on hope.

Contents

Joy is the emotional result of hope.
Peace is the emotional result of faith.
Love is the expression of both.

Introduction

Happiness is something that everyone desires, yet few know how to obtain. What constitutes true happiness has been a query that has captivated psychologists, philosophers and religious leaders for centuries. Many meaningful and insightful responses have been the outcome of the struggle to define and describe the elements that are essential to this universal pursuit. As a result, one thing has become clear. Happiness is not achieved by eliminating struggle. That should be encouragement to all of us, since life is filled with challenging and tumultuous times. Current events continuously make this indisputable. Mistrust and anxiety have crept into every crack in our social structures and are afflicting the very soul of our planet.

VUCA is an acronym that was made popular by the U.S. Army War College to describe the multilateral world that emerged at the end of the Cold War. VUCA stands for Volatility, Uncertainty, Complexity and Ambiguity. These characteristics have also become particularly descriptive of our post-pandemic world. Lack of clear and trustworthy information, disruption of supply chains, economic volatility, racial tension, political partisanship and international suspicion have all led to devastating levels of anxiety that have ravaged our emotional and mental health. The impact of these tectonic shifts in our society will be seen for years to come. The destructive surge of the resulting emotional tsunami will most certainly be significant, if not effectively addressed. People long for an end to the cascading calamities. We want stability. But a new normal and a predictable future don't seem to be a possibility anytime soon. Life as we knew it has changed forever. The last two years have scarred us in many ways.

If they ever come out with a Back to the Future IV, I am confident that somewhere in the dialogue Doc Emmett Brown will turn to Marty, while adjusting the flux capacitor, and utter these words, "I can't stress this enough, Marty. Don't ever set this to 2020 or '21!"

But here is the good news. In spite of present conditions and the dark clouds that loom on the horizon, there is hope. True happiness can be attained, even in the midst of struggles. By embracing time-tested principles and applying certain practices, you can craft for yourself a brighter tomorrow.

When COVID-19 began to entrench itself in the global psyche, a friend of mine suggested that I write a book that would help people weather what was sure to be an epic wave of physical and psychological challenges. He encouraged me to write a book on hope. I thought it was an interesting idea and accepted the challenge. Most of what I had read on the topic of hope was deeply rooted in spirituality. I understood well that the trilogy of faith, hope and love is a cornerstone of most religious teachings. However, I wanted to see if there was sufficient evidence to support the proposition that hope was fundamental to emotional health from a scientific perspective. So, I dove into the data. I found hundreds of scientifically-validated and peer-reviewed published research papers on the efficacy of hope. In the process, I found a very distinct causal link between hope and happiness. In fact, the data suggests that hope is an essential element to health, happiness, longevity and productivity. The science showed significant support for the hypothesis that hope and happiness are indeed linked.

This book is an attempt to synthesize and put into simple language the research on this link between hope and happiness. The principles set forth, and the applications suggested, are almost sure to elevate both hope and happiness. And, consequently extinguish the anxiety that so often accompanies times of volatility and uncertainty. COVID-19 is only one of many crises that will certainly occur in our lifetime. It serves as a vivid illustration of how fixated people can become on a problem and how quickly many lose hope. The ability to envision and create for oneself a brighter future, even in the midst of present dark conditions, is the hallmark of hope. Hope can effectively extinguish anxiety and set people free from the fear that can otherwise become debilitating.

It can rightly be said that happiness follows in the footsteps of hope. Every dream, every goal, every worthwhile endeavor and every longing must be sustained by hope. Without hope there is no passion to pursue positive change. Hope is foundational for emotional health. Hope keeps the soul afloat in tumultuous times. Hope can serve to protect us from the incendiary heat of hard times. Hope keeps the spirit aloft when facing the strong headwinds of adversity. Hope is transformative. And best of all, hope is available. Embrace hope and your life will be healthier, happier and more productive.

My hope is that this material will help you find happiness as you embrace hope for yourself. In the process, you will come to realize that you don't have to wait until life isn't hard before you make the choice to be happy!

Part One

PERSPECTIVE: YOUR VIEW OF THE CIRCUMSTANCES

ONE

The Great Pause

*The most intense conflicts, if overcome, leave behind a sense of
security and calm that is not easily disturbed.*

- CARL JUNG

It became one of the most widely circulated memes of the COVID-19 pandemic. It was a short, hand-written journal entry in an elementary homework binder. Schools were closed. Parents were scrambling to adjust to the new realities of life under stay-at-home mandates. On top of working from home, trying to safely secure needed food and supplies and deciphering the news, many parents were also being tasked with keeping their children's educations moving forward without disruption. It was a formidable task. Trying to keep a child focused on the school lessons at hand, while attempting to maintain sanity in the midst of the storm, many parents simply found themselves overwhelmed. One young student, by the name of Ben, captured the heart of the crisis in pencil. And he conveyed clearly what many were feeling. Here is how Ben saw and documented it.

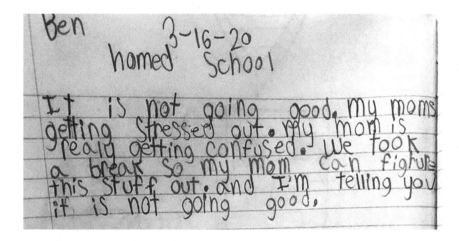

At some point, we've all felt like Ben. There are times when it just "is not going good." Life has a way of throwing us the unexpected. Things break. Dreams die. Promises aren't kept. Friends disappoint. Plans fail. Clients leave. Challenges arise. Investments are lost. Businesses go bankrupt. It happens. Sometimes it feels as if life is falling apart. In those times, we are challenged. It's hard to see life through any lens other than the one we are currently looking through. We need new glasses to see the world in a different way. Hope helps us gain a new perspective.

It's hard to see life through any lens other than the one we are currently looking through. We need new glasses to see the world in a different way. Hope helps us gain a new perspective.

When Life Pushed Pause

As I write these words, the world is undergoing a cataclysmic shift of seismic proportions. The date is April 1, 2020 but this is no fool's joke.

Life as we know it has changed. A single virus has put the entire planet on pause. A global pandemic has gripped our attention and robbed us of many of our freedoms. Its spread has been exponential. The death toll is rising and we have no idea when it may peak. It's a literal Sci-Fi horror flick come to life. Restaurants, bars, movie theaters and entertainment venues have been forced to shutter. Many will never open again. Public gatherings are strongly discouraged. Colleges and universities have been forced to move all classes online. Those who are younger are now being home-schooled, causing parents to scramble for solutions in order to stay sane. People have been forced to work from home. Travel is restricted and physical distancing is the new norm.

This week, the President announced that travel restrictions would remain in place for at least the next thirty days as we attempt to "flatten the curve" and contain the deadly COVID-19 virus. Borders have been closed. Empty planes are parked at airports that have become veritable ghost towns. Public transportation has been suspended and stay-at-home orders have been mandated widely. Weddings have been postponed. Funerals are being conducted online, leaving family and friends to grieve in isolation. A whole host of conveniences are no longer taken for granted.

Supply chains have been disrupted. A run on canned goods, paper products, hand sanitizers, thermometers and a wide array of other items have left many store shelves barren. Gyms, daycare centers, salons and service providers of all ilk have locked their doors. Malls and shopping centers have been abandoned. Routine office visits and elective medical and dental procedures have been temporarily banned. The global economy is straining under the load of widespread shutdowns and the worst is yet to come. Unemployment has skyrocketed to all-time highs and continues to soar upward daily. Those fortunate enough to have a job either risk exposure on the frontline or have been forced to work remotely, putting a strain on resources and relationships.

The healthcare system is stretched to the limits as the tide of cases continues to rise. Urban medical centers are bracing for the onslaught of new patients afflicted with the lung-crushing disease. Projections are complex and perplexing. Mixed messages are difficult to decipher. Extreme reactions abound as people contemplate what the future may hold. Anxiety and unrest have begun to infect the masses.

Tough times reveal what good times conceal.

One thing this crisis has confirmed is that tough times reveal what good times conceal. When life is good and challenges are few, we tend to become soft. We take things for granted. We don't appreciate the little things that make life sweet. Until tumultuous times come along, we don't deeply contemplate the nature of our relationships or adequately address factors that contribute to our emotional health and well-being. During good times we live distracted lives. We give little thought to the essential elements that anchor our lives and hold our souls steady in the storms.

When life is good, it's easy to become superficial. We can gloss over the uncomfortable issues that lurk just beneath the surface of our lives. We don't have to deal with our own demons when there are plenty of alternatives to distract us from doing the hard work of introspection. But when stay-at-home restrictions force us to face ourselves, many folks find they aren't comfortable with their own company. Issues that were previously concealed have now become clear. Our priorities and perspectives are now being challenged. The dark secrets of our distracted lives are now being revealed. Much like a beachball held beneath the water, our emotional issues eventually pop to the surface unexpectedly and oftentimes with great force. Failing to address these issues effectively will deeply impact us and will have a ripple effect on those around us. Because no one lives in isolation. This is true personally and it's true globally.

For the first time in a long time, we understand how crucially connected we are to everyone else on this planet. We see how the actions of a few can affect the many. We see that we truly are part of a global community. We are all connected and ultimately responsible for one another. We have come to realize, in a jarring fashion, the power of the human touch – both for harm and for healing. We have come to see just how fragile human life and connections can be. And, while the skies darken daily with new challenges, the less visible threats are even more disturbing.

Growing concerns over the impending healthcare strain and economic disaster are creating environmental conditions and relational tensions conducive to spawning an even more sinister storm. This new storm is as invisible and destructive as the novel virus, and much more distressing. It's the internal struggle that many are facing in the midst of these uncertain times. Loneliness, fear, anxiety and a sense of helplessness are infecting the masses. It seems to be spreading faster than the virus that caused these symptoms of an already sick society to surface.

Compounding the problem is the fact that people are physically distanced and emotionally disconnected. Current conditions are holding every human interaction somewhat suspect. Community gatherings are anathema. Neighbors now talk from a distance, if they talk to one another at all. Handshakes are all but a memory and hugs are out of the question, unless they are exchanged with those with whom you have been sequestered. Families are separated. Businesses are being run remotely. Relational tension is mounting for many. Human interactions are now relegated to the impersonal realm of technology. It's all talk and no human touch. The world has changed and we are all wondering if this may become the new norm.

The good news is that this will pass. In spite of what a few fearmongers may say, I can pretty much assure you that this is not the apocalypse. Dark clouds like these have occasionally gathered on the horizon throughout human history. In the last century, our forefathers had their own challenges to face. Some of us recall the World War stories told to us by our grandparents. The eldest among us still recollect the dark days of the Great Depression in the 1930s. There have been wars, natural disasters, terrorist attacks, bear markets and housing crashes that previously tested our mettle. But, thanks to the media, this is the first pandemic of such magnitude that it has created a global obsession. It's the first international crisis that millennials have seen in their lifetime. COVID-19 has sent a shock wave through society. The virus has indeed changed life as we know it. But the emotional and psychological fallout could even be more devastating. Many are unprepared to deal with the mental health challenges that are certain to come as a result of this crisis.

The Emotional Aftershock

Uncertainty can ravage the soul. This is especially true for those who are accustomed to controlling their environment in such a way as to get what they want. Now, the onus of control has shifted. The facade has been stripped away. Those who thought they were in control have been forced to admit that they are not. When that happens, many become nervous, if not unhinged. Some become desperate. The reality is the best one can do in the face of an uncontrollable pandemic is to be conscientious and responsible. Other than that, you have to let it run its course. All you can do is simply ride it out. Can it be curbed? Of course. Can we practice social distancing to "flatten the curve"? We must. But can we stop it in its tracks? Can we eradicate it? In time, maybe – but not likely anytime soon. And control it we cannot.

For some, this creates a sense of helplessness and hopelessness that can be debilitating. It makes many feel that life is vulnerable and left to the winds of chance. For the moment, the universe appears chaotic and cruel. The realization that control is an illusion is for some unbearable. For those who are addicted to control mechanisms, it is a gut punch that leaves them breathless.

Others struggle greatly with the realization that everything they worked so hard to acquire may now vanish as quickly as morning fog over a pond. For them, the sense of loss will likely run deep. Starting the climb over seems daunting and the ascent insurmountable. The emotional aftershock of this tectonic shift will be substantial. Stress, anxiety and depression abound. Hopelessness is creeping into the crevices of our souls.

How we choose to face and embrace the crises before us will determine our destiny. These times challenge our convictions. They test our resolve. And they reveal our values and the strength of our foundational beliefs.

How we choose to face and embrace the crises before us will determine our destiny.

You may remember the Allstate Great Recovery commercial, which first aired as the nation was reeling from the recession that rocked the economy in 2009. As it opens, Dennis Haysbert is shown looking out over downtown Los Angeles and says, "Years from now, how will we look back on today? As the Great Recession or the recession that made us great?" We then see a series of shots of Americans going about their daily lives, eating, riding their bikes to work, putting up new business signage; then Haysbert continues, "When the cars we built became smarter. When the houses we bought were meant for living in, not for showing off. When we remembered that living well meant living within our means. Allstate has seen 12 recoveries. But this one is different because *we're* different.

This was the time when we realized that our things are not as important as the future we're building for the ones we love. Protect yours. Put it in good hands."

It's a classic commercial. It poses a timeless question – a question that puts times like these into perspective. It's a question that should be asked again. *Will this be remembered as the Great Pandemic or the pandemic that made us great?*

Will this be the pause that finally gets our attention? For a moment, the treadmill has stopped. The daily grind has come to a halt and the streets are quiet. Life, for the most part, is unplugged. A few essential businesses are working feverishly to serve the masses that now have time to reimagine life and work. We have time to reflect. This is time that could be spent examining our basic assumptions. We could be investing in the relationships that have made life rich. But instead of doing the deep work of reflection and introspection, many are filling their days with worry and frantic activity. Some are obsessing on the news with its hourly updates. Connections are being strained and relationships are being tested. Eventually everyone will be forced to face themselves and address the underlying restlessness within.

There has been a wide range of reactions to this pandemic, offering a stark contrast. Some have found a place of peace and solace in the midst of this storm and others have fallen prey to a pervasive sense of panic. What accounts for this array of responses? Why have some been unshakable in the midst of the storm and others become unsettled? Why do some folks fold under the pressure forced upon them by uncontrollable circumstances, while others flow with the current of events and maintain a sense of calm and composure?

The answer, I believe, can be found in a word – hope. Those who have it are firmly anchored and can maintain sanity in the midst of the storm. And those who lack it are swept away and flounder in the fomenting waves of the tumultuous circumstances.

Storms will certainly come to life. Hope can help prepare us to effectively face these storms. So, whether you are currently weathering a storm or you're wise enough to prepare for those gathering on the horizon, the principles that follow can serve to anchor life as the surf surges. My hope in this endeavor is that you find helpful insights and practical solutions that will make your life better. After all, life becomes better when we become better at life. And we will become better at life by choosing hope.

TWO

Hope is the Best Strategy

Little minds are tamed and subdued by misfortune;
but great minds rise above them.

- WASHINGTON IRVING

This pandemic has caused me to ponder perplexing questions. What do you do when faced with difficulty? Why is it that when faced with seemingly insurmountable challenges, some people flounder or fold and others flourish? What's the secret to maintaining your sanity in the midst of the storms of life? What gives someone the courage to keep swimming when the currents are contrary and strong? In other words, how can we effectively navigate tumultuous times? How a person answers these questions will determine how well he or she deals with the realities of life in good times and bad. It will also factor in greatly to future success in whatever goals they may set.

No matter where a person may want to go and what they aspire to do, talent alone won't get anyone to a desired destination. Competencies count, but they are not all that's necessary to ensure success. This is particularly true in times of crisis. Sure, ability plays a role. But a wealth of research shows definitively that it's a person's psychological vehicles that predict success. Skill is important. However, the differentiating factor is someone's will. Does someone have the will and the emotional equilibrium to perform at a high level in spite of hardships? Core values and someone's psychological constitution will ultimately provide the foundation upon which the future is constructed.

Skill is important.
However, the differentiating factor is someone's will.

Over the years, a number of factors have been suggested to create a more positive outlook and elevate performance. Grit, Emotional Intelligence, Optimism, Mindfulness, Positivity and a slew of other concepts have been brought to the forefront to explain how to deal with life's harsh realities and build a brighter future. They're each important and their presence is certainly beneficial in explaining personal success to a certain degree. However, there is another essential element that I believe to be even more powerful. A critical component that is often overlooked. That's hope.

Hope often gets a bum rap. Sometimes hope is seen as simply wishful thinking when there is no evidence to support a particular position. Maybe the phrase, "hope against hope," comes to mind when expressing the sentiment that an idea is so far-fetched that it defies all reason. Some might say that hope is nothing more than possessing a Pollyanna attitude, subjugating reality in order to see life through rose-colored glasses. Others may cast aspersions when they declare, "Hope is not a strategy." This is most often taken to mean that without a defined destination and a clear means to get there, you are just wasting your time wandering through la-la land.

On the contrary, I would suggest that hope is not only foundational for all strategy – it is actually the best strategy. Without hope, there is little evidence that any strategy will work. Hope is most certainly a necessary ingredient to getting through difficult times. Hope is also elemental in order to accomplish any worthwhile undertaking. Hope must be present in order for any endeavor to be pursued with the commitment and emotional momentum necessary to bring it to fruition. But, before I set forth the case for its necessity, let's get a clear working definition of hope.

On the contrary, I would suggest that hope is not only foundational for all strategy – it is actually the best strategy.

It's Not Just Wishful Thinking

Hope is not merely a feel-good emotion. It is far more than an attempt to put a positive spin on bad circumstances. In 1991, Charles R. Snyder, and his colleagues at the University of Kansas, came up with Hope Theory. Based on his work, numerous studies have been conducted to link increased levels of hope to academic and athletic performance, as well as physical health and well-being. As Snyder's theory goes, "People who become 'high-hopers,' gain a more positive outlook on life."

According to Snyder, hope can be described as "the perceived ability to walk certain paths leading to a desired destination. It consists of goal-directed determination and planning of ways to meet goals."[1] In other words, no matter what you aspire to do, hope says that you can find a path to get to your goal. It's the belief that you can get there from here. Hope also provides the motivation when walking these paths. Hope consists of both rational elements and emotional elements. Snyder's Hope Theory includes goals, paths and freedom of choice. In simple terms, hope involves both possessing the will to make a specified goal become a reality and crafting the means in order to achieve it. It's the will and the way to make things happen.[2]

Hope is a dynamic motivational system tied to inspirational goal-setting. According to Snyder's model, hope has three components: goals, agency and pathways. Goals commonly refers to a desired outcome or a mental picture of a preferred future. Without goals life remains at a standstill or merely drifts. Agency is the ability to actively shape our lives. It's the belief that we can make positive things happen, accompanied by the motivation to reach certain desired outcomes. Pathways refers to the various ways one can get there. Pathways are the routes and plans that allow us to achieve the goal. Pathways also refers to the agility to change our course of action if one way is blocked.[3]

> *Hope is a dynamic motivational system*
> *tied to inspirational goal-setting.*

According to Shane Lopez, a senior scientist at Gallup and author of *Making Hope Happen*, "Hope doesn't relate to IQ or to income. Hope is an equal opportunity resource." And hope goes well beyond optimism. While optimism is a general belief that good things will happen, hope is focused on the accomplishment of specific goals. It's also the motivation to stay in the game when the going gets tough. Lopez has studied hope in millions of people through his work with the Gallup polls, and he has concluded that while hope and optimism are distinct from one another, both are important for happiness and well-being. While hopefulness alone doesn't make a person happy, it's a necessary step on the path to contentment, says Lopez. Hopeful people also have a greater sense that life is meaningful.[4]

Hopeful people share four core beliefs:

1. **Positivity:** *"My future can be brighter than today."*

   Hopeful individuals have a deep abiding conviction that no matter what today holds, tomorrow presents new opportunities. The dawning of a new day brings fresh possibilities. That's not to say that tomorrow will not present its own challenges, but rather that whatever may transpire, I'm not a victim of fate. I can act responsibly and conscientiously in crafting an approach to life and circumstances that opens up new ways of seeing and addressing the world.

2. **Responsibility:** *"I have a say in how my life unfolds."*

   Hopeful people have a deep-seated understanding that what happens in them is more important than what happens to them. I cannot control what happens around me, but I can be responsible for the way I react to those circumstances. The choices that I make and the actions that I take are critical. My inner world is more consequential for determining happiness and health than anything that may occur in my outer world.

3. **Agility:** *"I can find multiple pathways to achieve important goals."*

   Hopeful individuals are not limited to a few choices. With creativity and through collaboration, new means may be found to ensure that significant goals are realized. Often, there isn't a single "best way" to get things done. Usually, there are multiple routes that lead to the same destination. The key to success is often found in discovering these alternative routes when one pathway is blocked. The ability to be agile involves rallying the people and the resources needed to shift course when necessary.

4. **Your Reality:** *"I will encounter obstacles."*

Hopeful people are not naïve. They understand that there will be challenges. There are times in life that one will face substantial headwinds. That's acknowledging reality. I cannot expect life to be smooth sailing. That would be foolish. When the seas are high, it's necessary to adjust your sails and choose a new tack in order to maintain your momentum.

These four core beliefs serve to anchor life for hopeful folks in the midst of storms. This four-pronged perspective allows those with hope to effectively process and address whatever life may bring. Hope is neither soft nor passive. It has profound real-life ramifications. And hope plays an active part in creatively shaping the future. Having taken a look at the four core beliefs that form the underpinning of hope, let's now look at what this perspective produces.

The Active Side of Hope

"Hope is the basis of all positive change because hope is the belief that things could be better and one can make them so."

- SHANE LOPEZ

Hope is often mistaken for simply wishful thinking. The difference between wishing and hope is that wishing is passive and hope is active.

Wishing actually undermines one's chances of success. Wishing is associated with resignation. When we're confused or overwhelmed, a common defense mechanism is to withdraw emotionally and *hope* the problem will just go away. But that's not really hope; in fact, it's the opposite of hope. It's denial.

Hope involves the ability to envision a positive picture
of the future that you want and putting in the hard work
to turn desire into reality.

Hope involves the ability to envision a positive picture of the future that you want and putting in the hard work to turn desire into reality. This includes setting substantive goals, rallying resources and relationships, gauging progress and making needed adjustments until it happens. It's almost impossible to accomplish anything significant without being hopeful. When you believe that the future can be better than the present, then you start working harder today to make it come to fruition. You're much more likely to be engaged in the process and more creative along the way.

Of course, there are those rare cases where some folks seemingly stumble backwards into fortuitous situations. They rise to the top without any clear explanation as to how or why they got there. It occasionally happens. They find themselves at the right place at the right time and the winds of chance simply blow in their favor. They don't understand it. They cannot explain it. It's random. And it leaves everyone around them baffled and scratching their heads. But it's not a pattern that can be emulated. In order to build a better future, there must be intentionality. It takes a plan to make progress. And that's the difference between wishful thinking, or mere positivity, and hope.

It takes a plan in order to make progress. And that's the difference between wishful thinking, or mere positivity, and hope.

Hope has a plan. That plan has four foundational elements. Like the four points on a compass, they provide the orientation necessary to set a course and arrive at a desired destination. We will explore these components in greater detail later, but for the time being, here are the four functional elements of hope:

1. **The Work**

    The Work is the *occupational* part of hope. It is the *what* of hope. It involves both the destination and the doing. It points us toward an end goal. It's what you want to achieve. Most of us are inspired by meaningful goals. We want to be a part of something bigger than ourselves. We want to do good and make a positive contribution to a worthy cause. Even if we don't consider ourselves as having a particular mission, we all desire to be a part of making a difference in the world and leaving a positive wake in the lives of others. We also want to make our own lives better. We like to think that we have gained a certain sense of self-mastery that allows us to be the captain of our own soul. Meaningful work allows us to feel that our existence is impactful and worthwhile.

2. **The Will**

The Will is the *volitional* side of hope. It represents the *why* of hope. It provides the motivation to get the Work done. It is the agency. It is the energy, ethos, enthusiasm and passion that propels us toward the goal. Every endeavor involves both skill and will. The will is the fire in the belly, the grit and determination to get it done. It is the emotional equilibrium that prevents one from getting seasick and weary of doing well when the boat is being rocked by the waves of difficulty and uncertainty.

3. **The Way**

The Way is the *pivotal* part of hope. It is the *when*, the *where* and the *how* of hope. The Way speaks to the various paths that one can take in order to arrive at a given destination. It is the means by which one accomplishes the objectives necessary to reach a goal. Whenever obstacles are present, the Way involves the creativity to come up with a means to effectively clear or circumvent that which blocks the path. This creativity provides flexibility. Such agility must include reassessing and reimagining pathways to a desired destination when necessary.

Reassessing means that the goal must be evaluated in terms of a cost-benefit analysis. Sometimes the cost of attaining a given goal is too great to continue. When this is the case, the goal must be altered or the project abandoned altogether. If you choose to continue, then the goal must be reimagined. In such a case, a person must recalibrate in order to maintain a can-do spirit. An honest assessment may require someone to refocus toward a slightly different goal. At times, it may be necessary to re-goal. And re-goaling is where hope meets courage.

4. **The With**

> With is the *relational* side of hope. It is the *who* of hope. It refers to the people with whom you surround yourself in the undertaking of any task. It is the community with which you pursue a cause. This relational piece is crucial to the accomplishment of any goal. Courage and clarity come from being meaningfully connected to others who support our endeavors. Finding those who believe in you and want the best for you will provide the encouragement necessary to keep going when times get tough. Happy, healthy people are those who understand the power of strong relationships. They make it a priority to forge and nurture enduring friendships and partnerships.

So, hope is not passive. It is clearly strategic and it is much more pragmatic than you may think. When you are hopeful, you are deeply invested. Hope, then, involves setting an inspirational goal that you can pursue with passion. The pursuit of that goal will involve monitoring progress and adjusting course as necessary. It will include finding new means and methods to advance when you encounter challenges. And hope is either elevated or decimated by those that you choose to join you on your journey. Hope is not only the path to greater performance, it's also the means to a more meaningful and fulfilling life. Hope can change your life for the good.

THREE

Hope Floats

If you spend your whole life waiting for the storm,
you'll never enjoy the sunshine.

- MORRIS WEST

I've always enjoyed being on and around the water. From stream fishing and whitewater rafting to sailing on the open ocean, I have always found great pleasure in water activities. There's just something about standing in a mountain stream or riding an ocean wave that's both calming and exhilarating at the same time. The wind in your face and the gentle rocking motion of a catamaran on blue-green water is soothing for the soul.

In high school, I earned my certification as a Water Safety Instructor. As a lifeguard, I taught swimming lessons to pay my way through my first years of college. Later, I became a licensed Captain, capable of sailing vessels on the open seas. The primary concern of a lifeguard or captain is the safety and well-being of those under his watchful care. At a pool or beach, that means keeping an eye on anyone who may show signs of distress, with the preparedness to respond immediately if necessary.

On a vessel, that means ensuring that every passenger has access to a Personal Flotation Device (PFD). When waters get rough or there is imminent danger, it is essential that everyone be prepared in case of calamity. Should the vessel capsize or someone go overboard, each person must have equipment adequate to keep them afloat until help arrives.

In tumultuous times, life can become overwhelming and threaten to swamp even the best of plans. Sometimes circumstances arise, like a rogue wave, and pummel the least suspecting with challenges so severe that it can seem as if one is drowning. In such times, it is imperative that each person have access to an emotional flotation device. Emotional buoyancy is exactly what hope can provide. Because hope floats.

Diving into the Depths

If you're a strong swimmer, the best way to test the buoyancy of a device is to jump into deep water. As long as you can touch the bottom, you're not really testing the device. Once you're comfortable with the fact that you'll remain afloat in the deep, then you can begin to explore the various ways in which the device may be used to ensure safety in the shallows. In similar fashion, let's dive into the depths of a difficult discussion regarding extreme reactions to trying circumstances. Let's test which factors will keep us afloat in deep emotional waters. If our hypothesis stands the buoyancy test there, we can explore its efficacy elsewhere.

People have a wide array of reactions to stressors in life. For some, adversity is met with a steely resolve that perseveres through the pain. For others, the pain can become so excruciating that they consider ending life altogether. Vision for the future may become so clouded that some see suicide as their only option. Though it may be difficult to talk about suicide, there is a reason that I bring it up. If we can apply hope to shed light on this darkest night of the soul, then we can also apply those same principles to help us gain clarity when we encounter lesser challenges.

The absence of hope can cause depression. Depression can be described as the inability to find the motivation or the means to move life in a positive direction. Depression may be brought on by feelings of helplessness and hopelessness and may run the spectrum from mild to severe in intensity. In more severe cases, the individual may often feel unable to muster the energy necessary to attempt to make positive changes. They may feel as if their actions are meaningless and have no effect on the outcomes. For them, life is arbitrary and out of their control. They are victims of circumstance. They are acted upon, rather than being actors in how their life plays out.

The absence of hope can cause depression.
Depression can be described as the inability to find the
motivation or the means to move life in a positive direction.

To better understand how this thinking evolves, it's helpful to understand that there are both risk factors and resilience factors that play into a person's interpretation of reality. Risk factors contribute to someone reaching a point of despair so deep that they would contemplate ending life. These depressive symptoms could include stress, anxiety, loneliness, uncertainty and negative interpretations of events that would lead to a sense of hopelessness.[5]

In spite of the presence of these risk factors, some individuals still find the fortitude to deal with hardships in a positive way. It's worthwhile to look at these positive elements that motivate people to adopt coping strategies instead of suicidal behavior in the face of adversity. These positive constructs can buffer the kind of negative thinking that often leads to self-destructive behavior. For instance, there's an ongoing interest in exploring the concept of resilience and how it may minimize suicidal thoughts.[6] Resilience factors serve to moderate the risk factors which often manifest themselves in times of crisis.[7]

This moderating effect has led to a Positive Psychology movement that focuses on developing strengths and virtues that enable a person or organization to thrive. It has identified several resilience factors. One of these resilience factors is grit. Grit can be defined as "the extent of perseverance and passion in pursuit of long-term goals."[8] Grit is simply the intestinal fortitude to stick with a project or pursuit until it is attained. It's the ability to lower one's shoulder to the stone and grind it out until the task is complete. It's staying engaged, with an intense unwillingness to quit. It's the gumption to get it done. It's the focus to finish.

Grit helps someone endure life situations without losing focus on the ultimate goal, even if success is not immediately achieved. But grit also carries with it a caution. Grit is comprised of toughness and tenacity. And while that may keep someone's energy level high, grit can also cause someone to become so exclusively focused on finishing that he or she may ignore certain realities. Denial of pertinent details could be dangerous and lead to someone's undoing. For example, when I write a book, it's grit that enables me to spend hours upon hours writing. But if I were to ignore the research needed in the interest of finishing the manuscript, the very usefulness and value of the book would be greatly diminished. Grit must be combined with conscientiousness and responsible actions to be effective.

Gratitude is another resilience factor that has been extensively explored. Gratitude is a mindful appreciation of benefits and gifts that can be attributed to the kindness of other people. It can also be viewed in the wider context of noticing and appreciating what is good and positive in the world. Grateful people tend to have stronger relationships and a more positive outlook on their social environment. This, in turn, fosters a greater sense of belonging. Gratitude can offset feelings of isolation and the tendency to withdraw when times are tough. Social isolation and withdrawal are two of the final steps that lead to a decision to take one's own life.[9]

Gratitude involves an appreciation of the psychological and social resources that are available to someone. It renews an awareness of inter-personal support and connections, which can be immensely beneficial in combating depressive thoughts. But just how effective gratitude is in curbing suicide is still up for debate. Perhaps grateful individuals only experience resiliency when they also possess characteristics that help them persevere through challenging times. So, while gratitude may confer benefits for appreciating the good, a complementary psychological strength is needed to allow someone to persevere through the bad.[10]

Optimism is another resiliency factor. Dr. Martin Seligman is affec-tionately known as the father of Positive Psychology. Drawing from more than two decades of clinical research, he demonstrates how optimism enhances quality of life and how it can be learned. According to Seligman, your explanatory style is the manner in which you explain to yourself why events happen. An optimistic explanatory style can offset helplessness. Helplessness is the giving-up reaction; the quitting response that follows the belief that whatever you do will be ineffective. An ability to explain things optimistically can suspend feelings of helplessness, whereas a pessimistic explanatory style breeds helplessness. The way in which you explain events determines how helpless you can become – or how ener-gized – when you encounter an everyday setback or a momentous defeat.

Optimism can play a huge role in almost every area of life. Though not a panacea, it can produce a strong emotional defense against depression. It can raise one's level of achievement. It can enhance physical as well as emotional well-being. And it is a far more pleasant state to be in than helplessness. However, pessimism also has its own redeeming qualities when confronting reality. At times, you simply have to acknowledge that some things are impossible. In these times, it's best to refuse to foolishly continue their pursuit. Recognizing this, Seligman cautions against blind optimism and suggests a more balanced approach. Perhaps the greatest contribution to Positive Psychology that Seligman's research makes is to propose that optimism can actually be learned by challenging and changing one's inner dialogue.[11] It is not, as we tend to think, a personality trait that either you've got or you don't. Positive Psychology posits that one can plant and nurture the seeds of optimism where they don't seem to exist.

While optimism and hope are closely related, they are distinctly different. Optimism relates to how someone chooses to explain the cause of events. Optimism defines events in terms of three criteria: permanence, pervasiveness and personalization. Are bad events merely fleeting or are they here to stay? Are they limited in scope of impact or are they global? Am I solely to blame for their occurrence or are other factors involved? An optimistic outlook will tend to see bad events as temporary, limited in scope and impact, and may place the blame on factors outside of oneself. Optimism then clarifies the cause of past events and present conditions, while providing a general sense that the future can still be bright.

It could be said that optimism forms the foundation upon which hope builds the skyscraper, reaching for the heavens.

While hope and optimism are both important for happiness and well-being, optimism is only half of hope. Optimism serves to explain past events and present conditions. Hope, while similar in producing positive emotion, is more focused on building a brighter future through inspirational goal-setting and applying perseverance in finding a path to achievement. It could be said that optimism forms the foundation upon which hope builds the skyscraper, reaching for the heavens.

Grit, gratitude and optimism are all considered resilience factors in combating depression and suicide. However, research shows that hope, singularly and in conjunction with these other factors, is the most effective in fighting off negative thoughts and destructive behavior.[12]

Hope vs. Hopelessness

"Agency" is a sense of determination in achieving goals, which is the motivational component of hope. People with a high degree of agency thinking have a strong motivation and drive to achieve those goals, even in the face of hardship. "Pathways" is the term applied to one's ability to generate means and methods to attain established goals. People with high pathways thinking are more likely to generate a variety of routes that may be taken in pursuit of a goal, particularly if there are roadblocks and obstacles on the initial path. Conversely, people with low hope fail to generate alternate pathways either to achieve a blocked goal or to formulate new attainable goals. Low hope is characterized by having a lack of positive expectations for the future. Hope, then, is seen as the combination of determination and having a plan.[13, 14]

Aaron T. Beck and his colleagues developed a theory of hopelessness to account for depression. They defined hopelessness as the extent of negative attitudes about the future, particularly as it relates to situations or consequences that are largely beyond one's control. Interestingly, Beck's theory of hopelessness takes into account agency-like thinking, but the idea of goal pursuit is not considered.[15]

Beck's theory of hopelessness has been applied to better understand suicidal behavior. In a ten-year study, hopelessness was consistently shown to be one of the most predictive factors of suicidal ideation and eventual suicide. Persons with high levels of hopelessness misconstrue their experiences in negative ways and, consequently, anticipate dire outcomes resulting from their problems. Those with high levels of hopelessness eventually view suicide as the only way out of what they perceive to be an unsolvable problem.[16]

At first, it may seem logical to place hope and hopelessness on opposite ends of the same spectrum. However, they each have two distinctively different foundations. Snyder's hope construct is a goal-oriented model with two cognitive components: agency (the *Will*) and pathways (the *Way*). Each are essential to goal achievement. On the other hand, Beck's hopelessness construct is an overarching negative expectation regarding the future, without any consideration of specific goals or their pursuit.

Hope can shift our mental energy to attainable ends and brings new meaning and motivation as one reimagines the future.

Perhaps it would be better to see hope and hopelessness as two separate entities, each with its own range of intensity. This allows for a person to possess varying degrees of both elements at the same time. For example, a terminally ill patient may find joy and meaning in everyday life, while simultaneously experiencing pain, sadness and sorrow. In this scenario, hope is still possible even as someone faces a hopeless condition and imminent death. Even in such a case, one may still have a variety of goals. These goals may include seeking a cure, finding comfort, finishing life with dignity, leaving a legacy, increasing intimacy in relationships or something more spiritual like salvation. If one goal becomes unattainable, such as hope for survival at the terminal stage of an illness, then hope allows other goals and other pathways to emerge. Hope can shift our mental energy to attainable ends and brings new meaning and motivation as one reimagines the future.

Viewed as two separate entities, hope and hopelessness can interact with one another in four different combinations. These combinations result in either high or low likelihood of suicidal ideation. In these combinations, hope acts as a significant buffering agent in three of the four quadrants.

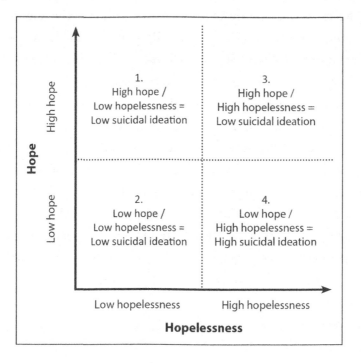

Low hope / Low hopelessness = Low suicidal ideation
High hope / Low hopelessness = Low suicidal ideation
High hope / High hopelessness = Low suicidal ideation
Low hope / High hopelessness = High suicidal ideation

*Those with high hope have more goals
and can envision more ways in which to achieve them.*

Thus, hope becomes a significant factor in offsetting the negative thinking that often leads to self-destructive activity. The resilience factor of hope mitigates the risk factor of hopelessness by reducing the likelihood of developing a poor coping style. According to Snyder's theory of hope, suicidal ideation is a result of perceived goal blockage. When a person fails to generate alternative pathways to achieve a blocked goal, or to reimagine a new attainable goal, then suicidal ideation may arise.

Those with high hope have more goals and can envision more ways in which to achieve them. When they encounter goal blockage or adversity, they have the ability to engage in "re-goaling." They generate adaptive coping strategies to accomplish new goals. High-hope individuals are less likely to develop suicidal ideation even when they are experiencing high levels of hopelessness because they can pursue other goals and rebound from their negative emotional state. Conversely, low-hope individuals who are at high levels of hopelessness are more likely to develop suicidal ideation because of the absence of hope in reducing the negative impact of hopelessness.[17]

*Hope serves to buffer a sense of hopelessness.
It is also a resilience factor, which can fight off the risk factors of
negative thinking and destructive behavior.*

It's fascinating to find that some people choose to end life under adversity, while others choose to take their hardships as a challenge and find new meaning and fulfillment in life despite high levels of hopelessness. I would submit that hope is a key factor in determining whether someone falters and folds or flourishes when tumultuous times come. Hope serves to buffer a sense of hopelessness. It is also a resilience factor, which can fight off the risk factors of negative thinking and destructive behavior. Although high hope individuals may still experience depressive thoughts and moods, they are likely to rebound by formulating new goals or finding new pathways to accomplish their goals when there is blockage. We have seen, then, that someone's level of hope moderates the relationship between hopelessness and suicidal ideation. Hope is a life preserver for those who may find themselves in deep water.

Hope is a life preserver for those who may find themselves in deep water.

Never Give Up. Never Quit.

On April 10, 2012, United States Army Staff Sergeant Travis Mills of the 82nd Airborne was critically injured on his third tour of duty in Afghanistan. While on patrol, Travis stepped on an IED (Improvised Explosive Device), causing him serious injuries to both legs and arms. Because of the heroic actions of the men in his unit, he was rushed to obtain immediate medical care. In spite of valiant attempts to piece his blown-apart body back together, Travis woke up from surgery on his twenty-fifth birthday as a quadruple amputee. He is one of only five soldiers to survive having lost both arms and both legs from the wars in Iraq and Afghanistan.

By his own admission, the initial days of dealing with the aftermath were difficult. The dreams of a young patriot and idealist had been shattered in an explosion that radically altered the course of his life. Physically, he was broken. Emotionally, he was devastated. His view of the future had been destroyed in the blast. In the quietness of the night, questions bombarded his mind like heavy artillery. How did this happen? Where was God? Will I forever be a burden and dependent on others? How is this better than dying?

Unable to walk or even feed himself, Travis was forced to reassess his life. He found little consolation in counseling. He knew there was no easy fix when you're taking fire. He was engaged in a battle for his soul and so the warrior within snapped to attention. There was something about his spirit that would not allow him to curl into a fetal position and quit. He was, at the core, a soldier and he was willing to fight for his future. As he lay in bed at the Walter Reed Army Medical Center, he began to recalibrate his expectations.

He had no arms. He had no legs. He had no idea what life might hold moving forward. But the one thing he did have was hope. He had his wife, Kelsey, and a beautiful six-month-old baby girl. He had the support and encouragement of other war veterans who had also conquered severe loss. And he had been given a challenge. So, he accepted the challenge. He began to reimagine his life after leaving Walter Reed. He adjusted the sights on his scope. He set new goals. The first goal was elementary. He wanted to learn to feed himself. His next goal was to walk again. It was difficult and painful, leaning heavily at first on the support of others. But he eventually did it. With each successive accomplishment, his outlook on life and the future began to grow brighter.

Today, Travis Mills is a recalibrated warrior, motivational speaker, author and advocate for veterans and amputees. His story is well-documented in his New York Times bestselling memoir, *Tough as They Come*. In September 2013, Travis and Kelsey founded a non-profit organization to benefit post-9/11 veterans who have been injured in active duty or as a result of their service to our nation. The Travis Mills Foundation provides all-inclusive, all-expense paid, barrier-free vacations to a resort in Maine, where they are able to participate in adaptive activities, bond with other veteran families and enjoy rest and relaxation in Maine's great outdoors. Travis found new meaning and purpose in life on the other side of devastation. His life is not defined by catastrophe. Rather, his life is anchored in hope.[18]

> *Hope fills your sails when the headwinds have left your life luffing. It sets a new tack to a new destination. And hope provides the buoyancy to prevent you from drowning when stormy waves swamp your dreams. Hope floats.*

Hope provides the motivation and the means to make life meaningful when it has seemingly fallen apart. Hope serves as a buffer to shield against the onslaught of negative thinking that often accompanies challenging times. When tough times come, hope makes you tougher. It increases your resilience and allows you to bounce back when life throws you to the ground. Hope fills your sails when the headwinds have left your life luffing. It sets a new tack to a new destination. And hope provides the buoyancy to prevent you from drowning when stormy waves swamp your dreams. Hope floats

Part One Challenge

GO TO: **FIREPROOFHAPPINESS.COM**

DOWNLOAD AND COMPLETE THE
LIFE PURPOSE STATEMENT GUIDE

Part Two

PROPHESY: YOUR VIEW OF THE FUTURE

FOUR

The Big Picture

You may encounter many defeats, but you must not be defeated.
In fact, it may be necessary to encounter the defeats,
so you can know who you are, what you can rise from,
how you can still come out of it.

- MAYA ANGELOU

I used to have 20/20 vision until I recently reached middle-age. Alright, maybe not so recently. But the point is that when I reached a ripe age, my vision changed. I began to see the ophthalmologist regularly. Every time I would go to her office, she would put this mechanical monstrosity in front of my face and proceed to drop a combination of lenses before my eyes. With each one, she would say, "One, or two? Better or worse?" She would continue the process until I could see clearly the letters on the chart. With each combination, my vision improved until everything was crystal clear.

We each see life through a complex combination of lenses. What provides clarity for me, may not provide clarity for you. The reverse is also true. There are the lenses of spouse, parent, team member, coach, friend, community leader and possibly boss. And the list goes on. There are also the lenses of your past experiences, your values, your present condition, your commitments, your inner voice and your expectations. The various combinations of these lenses will provide our view of the world. If these lenses are not combined effectively, our view can become distorted.

From Futility to Utility

When bad things happen, we have a natural tendency to want to know why. We reason that if we can explain it, then maybe we can control it. Or, at least, change it. But often, an explanation is illusive. Things just happen. Many of them are completely beyond our control. Diseases, meteorological storms, economic cycles and relational challenges are all a part of living on this planet. That makes us vulnerable. That makes us uncomfortable. If I cannot control my circumstances, then that makes me a victim of them, right? Not necessarily. Although some are inclined to play life out that way.

We can't control what happens around us,
but we certainly can be responsible for what happens within us.
We can be responsible for our responses,
our thought processes and our decisions in any situation.

The fact is there is much about life that you can't control. However, there also is much about life and yourself that you *can* control. We can't control what happens around us, but we certainly can be responsible for what happens within us. We can be responsible for our responses, our thought processes and our decisions in any situation. We can be conscientious about how we choose to play out our lives. We can be actively involved in making good decisions and moving in a positive direction that makes it much more likely to arrive at a desired destination than if we were to passively drift. Drifting rarely, if ever, allows you to reach a preferred place. If you want to be healthy and happy, you must remain at the helm and navigate tough times to the best of your ability. You can't emotionally abandon ship, or you'll be left in open water to be battered by the waves.

By staying emotionally engaged,
we can seek to find fresh meaning in
even the most difficult of circumstances.

By staying emotionally engaged, we can seek to find fresh meaning in even the most difficult of circumstances. Andrew Wyeth was one of the best-known American artists of the twentieth century. He was primarily a realist painter, working predominantly in a regionalist style. For the entirety of his seventy-year career, he rarely ventured outside of his home-town of Chadds Ford, Pennsylvania and his summer home in Cushing, Maine. In these two locations, he found his favorite subjects, which were the land and people around him.

Wyeth started drawing at a young age. He was a draftsman before he could read. When Andrew was a teenager, his father, Newell Convers (N. C.) Wyeth, brought him into his studio for the only art lessons he ever had and inspired his son's love of rural landscapes, sense of romance, and artistic traditions. He was a major influence in Andrew's life, fostering an inner self-confidence to follow his own talent without thought of how the work might be received. N. C. wrote the following in a letter to young Wyeth in 1944:

> "The great men Thoreau, Goethe, Emerson, Tolstoy forever radiate a sharp sense of that profound requirement of an artist, to fully understand that consequences of what he creates are unimportant. Let the motive for action be in the action itself and not in the event. I know from my own experience that when I create with any degree of strength and beauty, I have no thought of consequence. Anyone who creates for effect – to score a hit – does not know what he is missing."[19]

In the same letter, the elder Wyeth correlated being a great man with being a great painter: "To be a great artist requires emotional depth, an openness to look beyond self to the subject, and passion. A great painter, then, is one that enriches and broadens one's perspective."[20] The younger Wyeth grew up with a knack for finding fresh perspectives in his subjects. In a 1965 *Life* magazine article, he was quoted as saying, "My God, when you really begin to peer into something, a simple object, and realize the profound meaning of that thing – if you have an emotion about it, there's no end."[21] Wyeth was on a continual search to find profound meaning, even in the mundane. This meant looking long and deeply to view his subjects from different vantage points. He became obsessed with subtleties and perfected his ability to capture the not so obvious on canvas.

One of his favorite subjects was the Olson farm in Cushing, Maine. Here he created *Christina's World* (1948). Perhaps his best-known work, it depicts his neighbor, Christina Olson, sprawled on the dry field facing her house in the distance. Over the years, Wyeth created nearly 300 drawings, watercolors and tempera paintings at the Olson's homestead. Another one of his favorite subjects was German-born Helga Testorf. She was the subject of 247 of Wyeth's studies. Although Wyeth portrayed Helga as unsmiling and passive, he was able to capture subtle qualities of character and mood, as he does in many of his best portraits. This extensive study of one subject in differing contexts and emotional states is unique in American art.[22]

Perhaps what many people lack is the creative ability
to find new meaning in the mundane and messy aspects of life.
It could serve us well to look more deeply, or perhaps through a
different set of lenses, in order to see a different side of life.

Wyeth was often challenged by his critics to paint new subject matter. Yet, for the duration of his career, he stayed with the familiar scenes nearby. He didn't have to travel to exotic locations to expand his perspective. For him that would be easy, and frankly, quite boring. For Wyeth, there was great pleasure in seeking to find fresh meaning in the familiar.

There is much to be learned from N. C. Wyeth's advice to his son about being true to himself and not working for the effect. Freedom and confidence are often found in creating your own picture of the future, regardless of the circumstances and unconcerned with how it may be received. And from Andrew Wyeth himself, we are challenged to view a single subject from a variety of perspectives. In doing so, we may find something fresh. Perhaps what many people lack is the creative ability to find new meaning in the mundane and messy aspects of life. It could serve us well to look more deeply, or perhaps through a different set of lenses, in order to see a different side of life.

Fresh Meaning in the Messy

Life gets messy. It's hard to find meaning when you're in a quagmire. When you feel like you're in sinking sand, it's difficult to make sense of any situation. Tough times are tough to explain, particularly when they are due to no fault of our own. Of course, if we can connect our bad behavior to a negative consequence, then it is easier to draw lines of distinction and redirect our efforts to more productive ends. However, when life just happens and we find ourselves stumbling into a hornet's nest, it can be challenging to understand why. In these situations, it's more difficult to find anything good that could possibly emerge from the bad.

Perhaps it would be better to acknowledge
that while the reasons may elude us,
we can still leverage even the worst of conditions
to find meaning and beauty.

Some say that everything happens for a reason. This is often said in an attempt to make sense out of the senseless. But it never offers much comfort to those in the throes of devastating circumstances or after the loss of a loved one. Perhaps it would be better to acknowledge that while the reasons may elude us, we can still leverage even the worst of conditions to find meaning and beauty. Even when we can't explain why something has occurred, we can still find a lens that helps us look at life from an elevated perspective. Facing and embracing dark days can change us for the better. Obstacles can redirect us and set our lives on a totally different trajectory, if we confront them with hope.

With hope in the forefront, let me be so bold as to offer a few possible positive outcomes that could be ours if we choose to face and embrace the challenges that come our way.

1. **Challenges can prepare you for what is to come.**

    We've all heard that whatever doesn't kill you makes you stronger. There is truth in this statement. The only way to combat a virus is with an appropriate antibody. This antibody is made possible through exposure to the virus. Vaccines expose the body to small doses of the virus so that the body can build up an immunity. At the same time, exposure also has the capacity to build "herd immunity," which is the point at which a significant portion of the population has contracted a virus and recovered, rendering it incapable of spreading its harmful effects further.

    When we encounter challenges, it tests our mettle. The weight of the situation may be hard to lift. But when we do, it makes us stronger. It's just like lifting weights in the gym. The heavier the weight you lift, the stronger and thicker your muscle fibers become. The stronger you become, the more you are capable of lifting. But it's not just the amount of weight you can lift that counts. It's also imperative that you do the lifting with good form. If you lift weights improperly, you can do permanent damage. In the same way, you may be able to work your way out from under a crushing weight of devastating proportions. However, if you don't do it well, it can do damage emotionally, relationally and in a variety of other ways.

    When facing dark days, it's important to do the necessary heavy emotional lifting with good form. This means having the proper perspective to give you a stable base from which to lift. You have to maintain your emotional equilibrium in order to leverage your strength appropriately. Good form includes envisioning how the circumstances could be used to make you stronger. In order to make it through tough times, we have to have the ability to see ourselves on the other side of the situation. We have to believe that there will be another dawn just as certainly as the sun will rise again tomorrow. And, when that new day dawns, how will you see yourself? A healthy perspective is to envision yourself as bigger, stronger and better having gone through a strenuous workout.

A powerful realization that anyone can come to is the idea that present conditions may actually be conditioning you to be prepared for a brighter future.

A powerful realization that anyone can come to is the idea that present *conditions* may actually be *conditioning* you to be prepared for a brighter future. Workouts aren't fun. They can leave you tired and sore. But they create strength and stamina. These two qualities are necessary to compete at a higher level and come out victorious. You cannot experience the pleasure of victory without the pain of preparation. If you want to compete, you have to condition.

Tragedies occur outside of our control. That's part of life. You may never be able to make sense of it. We may never understand the reasons why someone dies, why we may be jilted for another lover or why an economic collapse or pandemic occurs. Sometimes, all you can focus on is lifting yourself out from under the pile of pain.

And it may be hard to find strength when all you are experiencing is the crushing weight of the circumstances. In times like these, it can be powerful to shift your focus. Work to improve your form. Change the way you choose to see the situation. Embrace the challenge and start to do the heavy lifting. You may not be able to lift the whole load all at once. Take it in manageable sets and reps. Most importantly, begin to see yourself as growing stronger in the process. You are in training. This is your conditioning to conquer the present circumstances and prepare yourself for what is to come. With hope, that means becoming stronger today and envisioning a brighter tomorrow.

2. **Challenges can make you more resilient.**

When I was a boy, one of my favorite toys was the Super Ball. Dropped from shoulder height onto a hard surface, a Super Ball would bounce back up to virtually the same level. No other ball could do that. And if you threw it hard against the ground, it would sky-rocket to exhilarating heights. It provided hours of playground delight as my friends and I challenged one another to see who could make it soar higher.

By contrast, Silly Putty could be rolled into a ball that would bounce if lightly dropped. But when thrown with force, it would break down and compress. And, when heat was applied, it would actually "melt" and liquify into a puddle. One of its characteristics is that it will conform to its environment, even lifting elements from the materials to which it is pressed. I would often press the pliable dough against the colorful comic strips in the Sunday newspaper. When flattened and then carefully peeled away, the putty would actually retain the comic on its surface. When under pressure, Silly Putty adapts to its surroundings and captures its content as its own. Its constitution is easily compromised and it conforms to its environment.

The Super Ball had a completely different constitution. The unique bouncy toy was formed out of a synthetic rubber invented in 1964 by chemist Norman Stingley. It was formed from a combination of compounds that gave it a very solid, yet somewhat flexible core. To form such a unique core, the compounds were vulcanized with sulfur at a temperature of 329 degrees Fahrenheit and pressurized at 3,500 psi (pounds per square inch). This provided the ball with a solid core and a nearly indestructible constitution.[23]

There is great benefit in having a solid core. A solid core produces resilience. This kind of solid core is constructed when high heat and pressure are combined. Values form the core of our lives. Our values are "vulcanized" best by the pressure and heat of constricting circumstances. Our values are forged through the refining fires of life. These values form the very basis of our behavior. What we value most will drive our thought processes and decision-making and ultimately direct our choices.

When our values are solid,
then the core of our lives will remain indestructible

When our values are solid, then the core of our lives will remain indestructible. One of the possible perceived benefits of difficult times is that it causes us to re-evaluate our values. A crisis can cause us to re-prioritize what is most important. Those things we once thought vital can easily become less valuable in times of coerced change. When our worlds are turned upside down, we are forced to reassess what is actually of value. Values may either be codified or transposed when they are tested. And that alone can be a very good thing.

Perhaps the most unique quality of a Super Ball is that when thrown down with a particular rotation, it will bounce back with a reverse directional spin. This cannot be explained by rigid body impact theory, and would not occur were the ball perfectly rigid.[24] This means that while the ball has a solid core, it is also quite flexible, making its bounce defy expectations.

When life throws us down hard in one direction,
hope gives us the ability to bounce back
with a totally different spin.
We aren't forced to go in the direction that we are thrown.
We can choose a different spin and bounce back higher.

While a solid core can provide resilience, flexibility is also essential. Where there is rigidity, breakage may occur as often as bounce. Flexibility in life allows us to shift course when necessary. This agility allows us to respond courageously to the unexpected. When life throws us down hard in one direction, hope gives us the ability to bounce back with a totally different spin. We aren't forced to go in the direction that we are thrown. We can choose a different spin and bounce back higher. Maybe it's time to put a new spin on the circumstances at hand.

One last fun fact to know and share about the Super Ball is that it was responsible for coining the name of one of the greatest sporting events on the planet. Lamar Hunt was the founder of the American Football League and owner of the Kansas City Chiefs. While watching his children play with a Super Ball one day, he came up with the term *Super Bowl*. He wrote a letter to NFL commissioner Pete Rozelle, dated July 25, 1966: "I have kiddingly called it the 'Super Bowl,' which obviously can be improved upon."[25] The league's franchise owners had previously decided on the designation of the *AFL-NFL World Championship Game*, but the media immediately picked up on Hunt's *Super Bowl* name. The new moniker became official beginning with the third annual game in 1969.[26]

The moral to the story is that if you want to compete in life's biggest games, like the Super Bowl, you have to possess both the solid core and flexibility of a Super Ball.

The moral to the story is that if you want to compete in life's biggest games, like the Super Bowl, you have to possess both the solid core and flexibility of a Super Ball. You have to possess resilience. And this kind of strength of core only comes by enduring the pressures and the heat of hard times. If we allow difficulties to do their work, we can develop perseverance and the resilience to bounce back with a new spin. Even when thrown down hard by life's forceful circumstances, with hope we can bounce back even higher than before.

The truth is that tough times never last.
But tough people do.

The truth is that tough times never last. But tough people do. Don't let the pressure of heavy challenges flatten you and cause you to compromise the core of who you are. Don't be like Silly Putty, conforming to the environment or taking on the negativity of naysayers. Rather, be more like a Super Ball. The direction you've been thrown is not the direction you have to go. When life throws you down, bounce back with a new spin. Tough times can make you resilient.

3. **Challenges can shatter bad beliefs.**

When something bad happens and the circumstances were a product of our own behavior, it has a big impact on our ego. Such a scenario can shatter our old beliefs and dismantle our preconceived assumptions. Failure provides a mirror in which we can see our unvarnished selves and be forced to confront those aspects of our character and conduct that simply don't work in real life.

Bad beliefs lead to bad behavior. The problem is that we all have blind spots, places in our lives where we don't see ourselves and the consequences of our behavior clearly. Sometimes we fail to realize the negative wake that we may be leaving in the world. Sometimes we simply don't slow down long enough to smell our own exhaust. We can be oblivious to actions and attitudes that do not serve us well. When this happens, then circumstances can easily turn against us. In these times, we are forced to reflect upon those elements in our character that need to be culled out.

Failure provides a mirror in which we can see our unvarnished selves and be forced to confront those aspects of our character and conduct that simply don't work in real life.

The painful realization that we have failed can be the very fuel necessary to precipitate change. Sometimes we have to be forced to look at things differently. Our beliefs are deeply ingrained within us. They're baked into us from an early age. With subsequent life experiences, our beliefs become codified. It's hard to overcome beliefs that we have held for so long. Until they fail us. Then, we have to do the hard work to pull them out by the roots. These beliefs frequently manifest themselves in self-talk.

John had come to believe that he offered little value to the world. As a young boy, he was criticized and rebuked incessantly by parents who lacked empathy. Raised in an environment that offered little emotional support, he grew up doubting himself. He was often depressed, withdrew from challenging activities and lacked the confidence to engage in social settings. When he experienced what he considered to be a failure or setback, he would regurgitate the same kind of conversation in his head that his parents initiated in his youth. He literally would demean and demoralize himself with his internal talk. Before anyone else was ever critical of John, he was critical of himself. This negative internal talk led him to some very dark places of the soul.

One day, over lunch, John confided to a colleague that he was struggling. Sensing that the issues were deeper than he was qualified to address, his colleague recommended that John see a counselor that he had met with on several occasions. To his credit, John made an appointment to see the counselor the following week. The counselor quickly identified the fact that John was living out his own self-fulfilling prophesies. He expected bad things to happen, so he began acting in such a way as to create the very situations that he feared. Because he told himself that he was unlikeable and unworthy, he withdrew from people. When people sensed him pulling away, they assumed that he wanted to be left alone and they pulled away as well. His bad beliefs about himself led to bad behavior. His negative expectations would then become a reality. Until he could see the world and himself in a different light, he was left alone to struggle in the darkness that he created for himself.

Fortunately, John's friend connected him with a good counselor. In time, John was able to face and change the way he spoke to himself. In order to move forward, his bad beliefs had to be broken down. Once his bad self-talk was called out, he was able to confront it. In time, he gained the tools he needed to challenge the conversations he was having with himself in his head. Slowly, his timidity was replaced with a willingness to step out and take risks. For the first time, he began to initiate conversations and build relationships. As his relationships grew, so did his sense of connectedness and emotional support. His depression began to fade away.

John made slow and steady progress. In the darkness of his depression, he reached out for help. With time and good counsel, John's beliefs were shifted. Life, as he had known it previously, wasn't working. It wasn't good. When he faced and embraced his bad believes, his behavior began to change. He started to speak better to himself and created a different kind of self-fulfilling prophesy. One that led to good.

Fighting an uphill battle that is
clearly insurmountable is the epitome of futility.
Sometimes you simply cannot gut it out or grind it out,
no matter how hard you may try.

This new view created positive results. New beliefs and more positive self-talk allowed him to step out of the shadows and engage with others. The more he engaged, the more affirmation and support he felt. As he gained more confidence, he began to move into relationships in positive ways. By allowing his bad beliefs to die, his bad behavior was eventually replaced with better choices. Those choices produced positive outcomes which, in turn, created a virtuous cycle that perpetuated itself.

4. Challenges can provide an opportunity to reimagine life.

Dreams sometimes die. Goals can get blocked. People can quit on you. Life can surprise you. When these things happen, it's easy to become fearful and fall back on primitive survival instincts. In bad times, some people fight and others take flight. Some respond to difficult times by heatedly engaging with whatever may be threatening to obscure their path. These fighters, though they may be valiant, often do more damage than good if their energies are misdirected. Fighting an uphill battle that is clearly insurmountable is the epitome of futility. Sometimes you simply cannot gut it out or grind it out, no matter how hard you may try.

On the other hand, when faced with daunting circumstances, some may tuck tail and run. They withdraw emotionally and physically. They may choose to stick their heads in the sand and seek to endure difficult circumstances through denial. These folks refuse to deal with the realities at hand. But postponing the inevitable never makes the situation better. Withdrawing and not addressing difficulties never resolves anything.

*Fighting, taking flight and freezing are all responses
born out of fear. Managing fear in difficult times is hard work
that never lets up. It is the work of a lifetime.*

Still others may do neither. The don't fight, nor do they take flight. Instead, they simply freeze. Like deer in bright headlights, they remain motionless, frozen in fear. They resign themselves to the perception that there is nothing they can do, so they don't do anything. Sometimes they simply stand still. Other times they may allow themselves to drift, taken wherever the winds of circumstance may blow them. They are the ultimate passivists. They assume no responsibility for their actions because they don't believe that their actions can actually make a difference.

Fighting, taking flight and freezing are all responses born out of fear. Managing fear in difficult times is hard work that never lets up. It is the work of a lifetime. As humans, we will always be hope-fear hybrids. Fear signals come from the part of the brain called the amygdala, signaling a whole-body response that gives us the resources to fight back, turn tail and run or play dead. Fear makes us behave as if we have blinders on. Our focus becomes narrow, seeing only the options immediately in front of us, and we lose our peripheral vision. When fear works, we momentarily escape what scares us. But the response can cause exhaustion and it comes with a whole host of negative emotional and physical consequences. When fear is at the helm, we find ourselves sailing in small circles. We fail to see the possibilities on the horizon. No creativity comes out of fear.

Hope takes the blinders off and helps us see opportunities.
When hope edges out fear, we find more pathways
to get to our goals.

On the other hand, hope springs from the part of the brain called the prefrontal cortex. When we attach our future to a goal that matters to us, our brain tells us to reach for it, finding the needed resources and support necessary to get the job done. In effect, hope takes the blinders off and helps us see opportunities. When hope edges out fear, we find more pathways to get to our goals. Innovation comes out of hope. We create something out of nothing. Hope broadens our thinking and fuels our persistence. Hope gives us the option of a fourth approach to deal with difficulties.

Creativity is what takes place when all the other options are taken off the table.

This fourth approach is far more promising. When faced with difficulties, you can choose to see a new-found freedom in the circumstances. Creativity is what takes place when all the other options are taken off the table. If life takes away an option, what other options can you possibly imagine? If one pathway is blocked, what alternative routes could you choose to take? You don't have to see challenges as a dead end. There are always options. Even if you find life pushing you down a one-way street, you can always alter course and use an ancillary route. If you suffer a setback or defeat, you can always start again. If you fail, now you have the freedom to try something new. How creatively can you reimagine ways to get to where you want to go?

*Focusing on progress rather than perfection
gives you the freedom to flow.*

One consideration that may be useful is to think in terms of progress and not perfection. Often, we construct for ourselves a picture of perfection. It's our way of imagining an ideal outcome to our efforts. However, circumstances rarely ever work out exactly as we expect. There are always potholes, speed bumps and detours along the way before we arrive at any destination. Its part of the journey. Rarely, if ever, do things work out perfectly. Focusing on progress rather than perfection gives you the freedom to flow without freaking out when life surprises you.

*Think about what would happen if you were to improve
any area of your life by just one percent every day.*

Think about what would happen if you were to improve any area of your life by just one percent every day. If you could focus on making incremental progress, it wouldn't be too long until you would see sizeable results. Often, we don't mark and celebrate improvement because we're too focused on perfection. When perfection is not achieved, we get discouraged. Pain jolts us out of the mistaken notion that we can ever experience the ideal here on earth. It is an illusion that we would do well to dismiss. Instead, strive for progress and appreciate the process. Celebrate the baby steps. Put one foot in front of the other and keep moving. Focus on the freedom that you have to make a choice to move in a different direction now that you've found one path to be blocked. And remember, it's not a dead-end, it's a cul-de-sac. This is your opportunity to turn around and find a new path.

Sure, you can be sympathetic, but empathy only happens when you can deeply relate to someone else through a common experience.

5. **Challenges can make you more relatable.**

It's hard to be empathetic when you haven't suffered through major defeat and tragedy. It's just true. Sure, you can be sympathetic, but empathy only happens when you can deeply relate to someone else through a common experience.

I used to think people who suffered from back pain were hypochondriacs, making a big deal out of nothing. That is until my back went out. It happened while I was spreading mulch in the front flower beds. At first, I couldn't wrap my head around the excruciating pain that pulsated through my body every time I made a minor move. After laying on the grass for over an hour to concoct an extraction plan, I was finally able to crawl into the house and find a comfortable place on the floor. I stayed there for the next two days until I could get a physical therapist to come save me from my plight. Since that experience, I have never made fun of someone with back pain again.

Hard times humble us and remind us that we too are human.
However, if we are wise, that humility can connect us
more deeply with the rest of humanity.

You know what I am talking about. That tendency to judge rather than to relate to others. We do it mostly out of pride. We don't believe ourselves to be vulnerable, while we may view others as weak. But pain has a tendency to equalize the playing field. Dark days remind us of our frailty and the unpredictability of life. Hard times humble us and remind us that we too are human. However, if we are wise, that humility can connect us more deeply with the rest of humanity.

Pain can also make you more real and far less superficial. We all want to put our best face on – our game face – the one we want the world to see. Our private face is the one that only those closest to us ever see. But our true face is the one we show no one. It is who we really are when everything else is stripped away. Our true face is who we really are at the very core of our being. Here we have to face ourselves and do the hard work of character development. This is where we become authentic.

Authenticity is being honest with yourself about yourself.
When you can be honest with yourself, then true change can
begin. Transparency is being honest with others about yourself.
And transparency makes you relatable.

Authenticity is being honest with yourself about yourself. When you can be honest with yourself, then true change can begin. Transparency is being honest with others about yourself. And transparency makes you relatable. Suffering has a wonderful way of stripping away the superficiality of life. Pain causes us to drop the pretense that keeps us distanced from others. Hardship welcomes you to the fraternity of humanity. You become more real and more relatable through rough times.

Suffering can ultimately make you more aware of others, when your focus is not all self-directed.

And, lastly, suffering can make you more sensitive to the needs of other people. Once you've been in the dungeon of despair, it's much easier to identify and relate to those who may be languishing there themselves. Suffering can ultimately make you more aware of others, when your focus is not all self-directed. Suffering creates sensitivity to the plight of others. That sensitivity can be used for good if you seek to create value for those who may be going through a similar situation. Once you've been there, you can shine a light for others and show them the way out. We live quite differently and much more happily when we no longer think the world should be ordered around us.

6. **Challenges can reframe your perspective.**

My mother was a strong Southern lady. She was loving, generous, resourceful and a wonderful cook. Unfortunately, I didn't truly appreciate her culinary skills until much later in life. Like most kids, I hated vegetables. As hard as I tried, I couldn't choke down her brussel sprouts, turnip greens and other green vegetable dishes. She would always say, "If I went to the trouble of preparing this food, then you're at least going to have the courtesy to eat a little of everything." And she meant it. I can remember being forced to sit at the table on a number of occasions in a battle of wills, until I succumbed and ate what was on my plate.

On one occasion, I was particularly belligerent. She finally pulled out the old guilt trip statement, "You know, there are starving children in other parts of the world who would be thankful to have food to eat." It wasn't the first time that she had used that line. And this time I was ready with my response. When she finished speaking, I reached into my pocket and pulled out six stamps. "Great," I said, "Here are enough stamps to mail it to them!" I don't need to tell you the rest of the story. Suffice it to say, it did not go well for me. Her statement didn't change my perspective, but a belt certainly did. Sometimes a *good ole whoopin'* can change your perspective.

Whenever I am emotionally down or seriously discouraged, I have a good friend I call to help me process the situation. He serves as a sounding board and checks my thinking. He listens intently as I bemoan my plight. He patiently takes it all in, as I explain in great detail what I am going through. He asks a few clarifying questions and always expresses empathy. Then, he offers his best advice for my consideration. He is a good friend who provides emotional support and wise counsel. He has an objective way of helping me see life more clearly when I am in the midst of a crisis.

On one distinct occasion, after having poured my heart out for a considerable period of time, he asked, "Do you want my honest assessment?" "Of course, I do. That's why I called you." Letting my response hang in the air long enough for me to own it, he then said, "This all sounds like a First World problem to me." I knew immediately what he was saying. He wasn't referring to First-World in a geopolitical sense. Rather, he was making a comparison in contrast to Third World, meaning poor and underdeveloped.

I have visited Third World countries on numerous occasions. I have witnessed the poverty and depravity. Life there can be raw and rough. I have seen communities that lacked running water or a sanitary means to remove waste. I have seen children without food and clothing. I have witnessed teens running through dusty streets without shoes. I have witnessed what happens when there is a lack of medical care. Life can be desperate in places like that.

A crisis can become a catalyst for change.
Challenging times have a way of teaching life lessons
you may have never learned voluntarily.

My friend was making a point. I have food. I have clothing. I don't lack for shelter or running water. Sometimes, it helps to remember that our problem may pale in comparison to what so many others on our planet have to face on a daily basis. It helps to put our problems into perspective. This is not to say that our challenges are not real, or painful or daunting. But it does make you stop and think about the riches and resources that we do have compared to so many. And that realization alone can put a whole new spin on how we think about them and how we address them. If we are honest, many of our problems could be classified as First World challenges.

A crisis can become a catalyst for change. Challenging times have a way of teaching life lessons you may have never learned voluntarily. Every crisis is an invitation to become more than you currently are. If you choose to face and embrace the challenges that come your way, then there is immeasurable good that could come from bad circumstances. The question is whether or not you will be able to envision the opportunities beyond the obstacles. Will you allow the challenges of life to change you for the better? Or, will you allow difficulties to grind you into dust? How you choose to explain life events and how you deal with difficulty will determine your destiny. People who choose hope, choose to move forward, find new paths and take responsibility for making life better.

Hope helps you to see the big picture.

Remember Ben's poor mother in chapter one? She was having a hard time figuring out home-schooling in the midst of the quarantine. But at least she had the wisdom to take a break and attempt to, as Ben said, "figure this stuff out." Let's hope that she was able to come back with a fresh perspective that served them both well. At least, I would like to imagine things eventually working out that way. In times of crisis, it would serve us well to take a break and try to figure stuff out. In so doing, perhaps we can imagine the good that could possibly come from the bad, if we can only approach challenges with a fresh perspective. Hope helps you to see the big picture.

FIVE

Building the Case for Hope & Happiness

He who is not every day conquering some
fear has not learned the secret of life.

- RALPH WALDO EMERSON

ope as a functional construct in real life may be a bit difficult for some to grasp. Hope may sound even more fuzzy when applied as a leadership concept. While hope may initially appear to be a soft idea, it has hard-edged, bottom-line implications for life, relationships and business. The more clearly hope is defined and the more practical we make it, the more powerful it becomes. In other words, there must be validity and utility in order for the concept of hope to be a viable strategy for dealing with relevant life issues.

Over the past two decades, there have been hundreds of studies done on hope. Charles Snyder's work around his Hope Theory ignited a firestorm of research on the impact that hope can have on everyday life. Since then, studies have been conducted showing the effect of hope on academic and athletic performance, sales productivity, longevity, leadership effectiveness, creativity and problem-solving capacity, as well as health and happiness. The list could go on and the research, as well as results, are most impressive.

Hope isn't just for dreamers and poets. Hope is for doers. Hope makes a difference in how we make daily decisions and is a clear predictor of long-term success and happiness.

Hope isn't just for dreamers and poets. Hope is for doers. Hope makes a difference in how we make daily decisions and is a clear predictor of long-term success and happiness. It happens to be much more pragmatic than most might think. It can also be contagious, changing relationships and leading to personal and cultural transformation. Let's look at the impact that hope can have in a variety of settings, when it's fully understood and embraced.

Hope and the Workplace

A focus on hope, and its ability to enhance the workplace, is significant because of the increasingly dynamic work environments that teams face today. From mergers and acquisitions, downsizing, bankruptcies, advancing technologies and a highly competitive and volatile global marketplace, employees are facing continuous and rapid change. Today's work environments require people to be agile and adaptive to effectively manage their careers.

There has been a significant shift away from traditional organizational career-pathing to an emphasis on job-crafting. Job-crafting is the ability to be responsive to work qualifications and expectations, as well as pursuing continuing training and the development of competencies to meet work demands. The present-day workplace presents challenges and obstacles that can only be met by those who demonstrate mastery of positive psychological components. Hope contributes significantly on several fronts.

Low-hope engineers cost the firm nearly four times more than their high-hope colleagues in lost productivity.

For starters, hopeful workers show up for work. A study conducted by James Avey, of Central Washington University, proved that workers who were excited about company goals and their own future missed less work. Avey and his colleagues studied hope and absenteeism among more than one-hundred mechanical and electrical engineers in a Fortune 100 high-tech firm. The test group was a representative sample of the company's 179,000 employees. They found that those assessed to be high-hope engineers missed, on average, less than three days of work (not including planned leaves or vacations) in a twelve-month period. In fact, many of them missed no time at all. This was significantly better than their low-hope counterparts, who missed more than ten days of work each, on average, in the same period of time. The result was that the low-hope engineers cost the firm nearly four times more than their high-hope colleagues in lost productivity. Compared with a number of other factors (including job satisfaction, confidence to do the job and company commitment), no other workplace measure counted more than hope in ascertaining whether an employee shows up. And, of course, we all know that showing up is half the job. It can be stated with confidence that hope curbs absenteeism.[27]

Additionally, it has been shown that hopeful workers are more engaged. In addition to simply showing up, high-hope folks are far more involved and enthusiastic about their work. This is significant since research from the Gallup organization has confirmed that well over sixty percent of the American workforce is either not engaged or actively disengaged. This lack of engagement leads not only to absenteeism, but also to mediocre performance and workman's compensation claims brought about by injuries due to inattentiveness on the job. Hope mitigates risk and increases engagement.

Hope and Productivity

Business professor Suzanne Peterson, of Arizona State University, presented a challenging scenario to executives at a top financial services group. Here was the imaginary dilemma:

> "Imagine showing up for work and finding out that your colleague has left the company and you have to take her place as a project leader. Your new team is charged with solving a problem that has been hitting the bottom line hard. Your boss is quick to emphasize the importance of the project and to point out some major obstacles that you will encounter: one team member will undermine your authority; you need more team members but don't have the budget to hire them; your leadership style differs from your predecessor; you report to two supervisors; and you

aren't completely clear on which steps to take first because you receive conflicting information from various sources."[28]

Hope is especially important in organizations experiencing uncertainty due to rapid changes in focus and shifts in leadership.

Quite the conundrum, right? Peterson gave each executive two weeks to come up with as many high-quality solutions as possible for this complex problem. She was interested in discovering how hope was associated with the quantity and quality of problem-solving strategies proposed by each participant. She assessed each executive using a hope scale and she coalesced a panel of supervisors to blindly rate the quality of the submissions. With data in hand, Peterson found that the more hopeful executives produced better results. They also submitted more solutions, which she surmised may have indicated that they felt some of the solutions may not have been viable.

Peterson noted that hope is especially important in organizations experiencing uncertainty due to rapid changes in focus and shifts in leadership. According to her, "It may be these settings where employees' hopefulness can have a greater impact because they require the problem-solving orientation and perseverance of those with higher hope."[29] Similarly, in another study, Peterson found that hope was a more powerful predictor of performance in start-up ventures than in more established organizations. She observed that this is likely the case because, "hopeful employees are more likely to engage in and accept organizational change efforts."[30]

The hope-productivity link has been consistently demonstrated in numerous studies targeting a variety of outcomes, across many different professions around the globe. Hopeful salespeople reach their quotas more frequently, hopeful mortgage brokers process and close more loans, and hopeful executives meet their quarterly goals more consistently. Whenever researchers have assessed the relationship between hope and performance, they have found a meaningful link.

People who believe that they are part of something bigger,
that they are making the future better for themselves and others,
will simply get more done.

Consider a study of Quick Service Restaurants. Fifty-nine managers, from a nationally known fast-food chain, were ranked from low to high on a self-reported hope scale. Then researchers paired data on each franchisee's overall profitability with the manager's level of hope. The high-hope managers were significantly more profitable than the low-hope managers. And the trend held true for employee turnover, which is a crucial metric for anyone in the service industry.[31] People who believe that they are part of something bigger, that they are making the future better for themselves and others, will simply get more done. High hope people are the difference makers in our modern economy.

It appears likely that this hope-productivity link is established early on when people are still in school. Hope has effectively predicted academic performance of students in elementary school through post-graduate studies. Hope can be linked to increased test scoring and term GPA. Four longitudinal studies have provided compelling evidence for the added value of hope. These long-term studies show how the passage of time influences the link between hope and academic success. Three of these studies followed college students from their freshman year to their graduation or attrition. The fourth study was conducted with first-year law students.

The setup for each study was simple. Researchers gave each student a standardized assessment, measuring their level of hope, and they requested access to their personal school records for some years to come. Researchers then unobtrusively monitored their progress academically until they either graduated or dropped out of school. Statistical models were then used to correlate the data. Each study controlled for the other determinants of school success, such as GPA at previous academic levels and entrance exam scores.

The results from studies conducted both in the United States and the United Kingdom were almost identical. In each study, the findings were clear. The more hopeful students were about their future, the better their academic performance. How students thought about their future predicted benchmarks of academic progress and success. Hope was found to be linked to how many courses they enrolled in, how many credit hours they earned, their GPA across those courses, their cumulative GPA and the likelihood that each would graduate. What was particularly noteworthy was that one study showed that low-hope students were three times more likely to be dismissed from school because of poor grades. Another study found that hope was a better predictor of ongoing enrollment and graduation than standardized entrance exams like the ACT.

The study that provided perhaps the most surprising results was the one conducted on law students. Undergraduate GPA and Law School Admission Test (LSAT) scores were collected, as well as a hope measurement taken, when each student entered the program. The hope scale predicted success during the first semester, which is considered by most to be the most stressful. When predictors were ranked from strongest to weakest, it was determined that a student's undergraduate GPA was the best predictor. However, hope was a better predictor of final law school ranking than the LSAT. This result was shocking![32]

Other conditions being equal,
hope leads to a twelve percent gain in academic performance,
a fourteen percent bump in workplace outcomes
and a ten percent boost in happiness.

Shane Lopez and his associates have conducted three meta-analyses, examining the results of over one hundred hope studies. Drawing from psychologists and educators from around the globe, they have pulled together research on how hope relates to academic performance, business outcomes and well-being. Their work clearly shows the science of hope. How we think about the future is a key determining factor of success in school, work and life. Other conditions being equal, hope leads to a twelve percent gain in academic performance, a fourteen percent bump in workplace outcomes and a ten percent boost in happiness. To put it simply, a typical group of high-hope students will score a letter grade higher than their low-hope peers. A group of high-hope sales people will sell more product in six days than their low-hope colleagues will sell in seven. That is a substantial increase for anyone looking to elevate business outcomes. To top it off, high-hope people are just plain happier than their low-hope friends. Happy people create a better workplace and do better work.

If you are an individual seeking to improve your performance, you may want to consider what hope could do for you. If you are an executive or a leader of teams, you might want to explore how a hopeful culture could enhance your bottom line. The possible benefits of embracing hope as a strategy are numerous. And science is proving the results.[33]

Hope is a requisite skill for leadership.
It is critical to effective management as it engenders a culture
of engagement, where employees are productive
even in the face of uncertainty and adversity.

Hope and Leadership

So, what implications does all of this have for the impact of hope on leadership? It turns out that the connection is profound. This is particularly true in the midst of chaos and uncertainty, which is often brought about by significant change. If you are a leader, it is imperative that you foster an environment fraught with hope. Hope is instrumental in creating a compelling culture.

Hope is a requisite skill for leadership. It is critical to effective management as it engenders a culture of engagement, where employees are productive even in the face of uncertainty and adversity.

When everything else is out of control, engagement is one thing
that a leader can directly influence. This engagement can be
enhanced by consistently applying four leadership principles:
transparency in all matters; making necessary changes quickly;
constant and clear communication with team members;
and instilling hope.

Despite limited resources, structural changes, redundancies and declining real pay and benefits, organizations that foster hope are able to maintain higher levels of employee engagement. It turns out that when everything else is out of control, engagement is one thing that a leader can directly influence. This engagement can be enhanced by consistently applying four leadership principles: transparency in all matters; making necessary changes quickly; constant and clear communication with team members; and instilling hope.

Transparency breeds trust. It's that simple. Authenticity is the ability to be honest with yourself about yourself. Transparency, similarly, is being honest with others about yourself and the situation. Leaders may be tempted to put a good spin on a bad situation. They may think that by distorting the facts, they are shielding folks from harsh realities in order to protect them from becoming discouraged. But in doing so, they are merely putting lipstick on a pig – it doesn't make the prospects look any better. Rather than engendering trust, they create just the opposite effect. They lose both the respect and trust of those in their ranks.

Pivoting means keeping one foot firmly planted,
while moving the other to gain an advantage.

When news is bad, disclose it. Of course, you have to do it appropriately. But when people have a clear picture of the issues at play, then they can choose to be an active part in coming up with a solution. Strong teams will rise to the occasion, if given the opportunity. Good teams want to know exactly what they are up against. When the details are fully known, they can be challenged to rally around a common cause and utilize their creativity. Challenges can be a catalyst, causing teams to work collaboratively to solve the problems at hand.

In hard times, speed and agility are also essential. Holding steadfastly to a clearly blocked goal, or keeping your saddle on a dying dream too long can be costly. Leaders must be able to pivot in order to continue to provide value for customers both internally and externally. Pivoting means keeping one foot firmly planted, while moving the other to gain an advantage. This understanding is crucial. Keeping one foot firmly planted means that you never abandon your purpose. Your product or offering may change, your go-to-market strategy may morph, and your resources may be realigned to meet demand. But your purpose must remain solid and unshifting. Many a company has lost their way by holding tight to a product and losing sight of or neglecting their purpose.

Kodak is a classic example. A technology company that dominated the film market during the twentieth century, Kodak's leaders blew its chance to lead the digital photography revolution because they were in denial for too long. Though the company actually invented the first digital camera back in 1975, the leaders of Kodak failed to see digital photography as a disruptive technology. They refused to pursue it for fear of the negative effects on the film market. Management was so focused on film sales that they missed the digital revolution, after having started it. Consequently, Kodak filed for bankruptcy in 2012. They could have pivoted around their purpose of "capturing everyday moments and memories," by applying new technologies. Instead, they attempted to preserve a product and pivoted away from their purpose to their own demise.

Additionally, constant and clear communication is vital in maintaining transparency. Where there is a vacuum in communication, people will tend to fill it by expecting the worst, rather than believing the best. People, by nature, suffer from loss aversion. We tend to believe that it is better not to lose five dollars than to find five dollars. This loss aversion causes us to set up negative expectations in order to build defenses against loss. So, when there is inadequate information, people tend to make projections that are negative and exaggerated. Knowing this, good leaders speak with conviction and clarity. Bad news, as we have said, is better than no news. People can cope with negative news better than uncertainty. Clear and consistent communication is critical, especially during times of chaos or change.

And lastly, the ability of a leader to instill hope is paramount. Hope provides a challenged workforce with a sense of stability, trust and compassion. Leaders who instill hope are much more able to keep their team members happy, motivated and committed. A leader who expects the future to be better and brighter will naturally work diligently to achieve established goals, believing that the team can greatly influence the outcomes.

Hope, Health & Happiness

Hope may feel good, but it's also good for you. According to well-being expert Ed Diener of the University of Illinois, someone who is satisfied with life, experiencing positive emotions, and not experiencing negative emotions meets the basic criteria for a happiness diagnosis.[34]

Shane Lopez and Matt Gallagher of Boston University wanted to see if there was a link between hope and happiness. They asked people if they were hopeful and satisfied with their lives, then measured the presence of good feelings and the absence of bad ones. They wanted to know if being hopeful predicted (or was predicted by) these symptoms of happiness. Hope proved to be a strong and unique predictor of satisfaction and positive emotions.[35]

Correlational findings, including anecdotal data and poll results, suggest that happiness and hope do indeed go together. The two are inextricably tied together. The question, however, is how do they relate to one another? Does one cause the other or do they simply tend to appear together?

Hope buffers the effects of negative life events and shields from stress and sadness, making room for happiness.

Research appears to suggest that hope actually induces higher levels of satisfaction. Longitudinal studies of workers have suggested that high-hope employees experience more well-being over time. Hope buffers the effects of negative life events and shields from stress and sadness, making room for happiness. In a study of firefighters coping with the daily stress inherent in their jobs, those first responders with the highest levels of hope were able to protect themselves far better psychologically from the stress that can accumulate over an entire shift.[36]

Additionally, our thoughts about the future may do more than buffer us from the bad in life. Hope may also contribute directly to finding deeper meaning and purpose, leading to well-being. Studies by psychology professor David Feldman of Santa Clara University showed a correlation between hope and meaning that was the highest for any factor associated with hope. Perhaps one of the greatest benefits of hope is that it compels us to pursue what matters most, which gives us a sense of control and purpose that is instrumental to well-being.[37]

Research has established a strong connection between hope and happiness. We can say with certainty that hope is an essential element in producing happiness. What is also clear is that meaning and fulfillment in life do not exist apart from hope. Hope, apparently, is the secret sauce to satisfaction and happiness.

What is also clear is that meaning and fulfillment
in life do not exist apart from hope.
Hope, apparently, is the secret sauce of satisfaction.

Rick Snyder, as a part of his work on Hope Theory, also did work from the opposite end of the spectrum – showing the connection between hope and pain. One of his studies showed that hopeful people tolerated pain almost twice as long as people who were less hopeful. This finding has now been replicated in numerous controlled experiments. These coping studies have sparked research into how hope could promote healthy behaviors, including regular exercise, safe sex practices, moderation in drinking, quitting smoking and consuming fruits and vegetables. In each case, hope for the future is clearly linked with daily habits that support health and prevent disease. People with high levels of hope tend to make better choices when it comes to their health.[38]

The same is true for people who are managing chronic health conditions. Professor Carla Berg of Emory University wondered if hope in young asthma patients was associated with adherence to their treatment regime of daily inhaled steroids. Those patients, diagnosed with moderate to severe asthma, completed a youth version of the hope scale and were directed to take their medication as prescribed. With controls in place, Berg tracked their compliance by electronically monitoring each child's metered dose over a fourteen-day period. Then, she examined the relationship between adherence and variables, including demographic characteristics. Among all the factors studied, a child's hope was the only significant predictor of which patients followed the doctor's orders.[39]

Hope and Longevity

Stephen Stern, professor at Psychiatry, along with scientists at the University of Texas Health Science Center in San Antonio studied mortality in older members of the local community. They wanted to find out why some people die while others, who may be no less ill or in no less physical danger, continue to live. Finding the answer would require tracking a large group of people over an extended period of time, accounting for the many factors that may undermine each person's health.

Stern took a group of 795 San Antonio residents, ranging in age from 64 to 79, who had taken part in a large prospective study of heart disease that began in 1979. Between 1992 and 1996, the participants added to their extensive research by completing tests measuring cognitive performance as well as health markers (such as medical history, blood pressure, body mass index), lifestyle factors (such as drinking, smoking and exercise) and extent of social support.

Stern and his team set out to determine if hope could be considered a matter of life and death. Included in the home-based assessment was a simple question: "Are you hopeful about the future?" When the responses were tallied, 91% answered "yes," while only 9% said "no." The two groups were equally matched in terms of ethnic makeup and sex. These two groups were of similar educational background and were in comparable health. At the time of the first home visit, participants showed no significant differences in blood pressure, body mass index or drinking behavior.

However, there were some notable dissimilarities. Many more of the hopeful were rated "high" in physical activity (48%, as compared to 28%). Fewer were current smokers (15%, versus 25%). The higher-hope individuals scored much lower on a standard measure of depression and significantly higher on measures of social well-being, with a higher number of people in their network of relational support.

*How we think about tomorrow directly influences our behavior
today. And better behavior today leads to a brighter tomorrow.
Hope is a principle ingredient in happiness,
health and well-being.*

After their intake, the participants were told nothing about their results and they received no recommendations for health care or interventions moving forward. They were left to lead their lives as they would so choose. Meanwhile, the researchers were monitoring the development of the two groups from a distance. Participants were tracked through a variety of means. Deaths were counted and diseases classified. By August 1999, the results were clear. Of the small group that had classified themselves as hopeless, 29% had died, compared to only 11% of the hopeful participants. There were no suicides, but cancer and heart attack had claimed 2.8% of the hopeful, compared to 7.2% of the hopeless.

When all of the other factors were considered, people who said they felt hopeless were almost three times as likely to die during the follow-up period as those who said they were hopeful about the future. The results were striking. According to Stern, the link between hope and longevity is "behaviorally mediated." In other words, those who have hope for the future are driven to particular behaviors in the present. Those behaviors, in turn, result in a longer life.[40]

As we have seen, hope is not an attitude or belief that benefits us in some mysterious way. As Lopez says, "Hope can lift our spirits, buoy our energy and make life worth living."[41] It also changes the way we see life and impacts our daily choices. How we think about tomorrow directly influences our behavior today. And better behavior today leads to a brighter tomorrow. Hope is a principle ingredient in happiness, health and well-being.

Hope and Positivity

I'm a big believer in the power of positivity. I would much rather spend my time around optimistic people than nay-sayers. I am so optimistic, in fact, that my wife occasionally jests that I live in la-la land. There is probably some truth to that. But I'd much rather live in la-la land than in a Pity Party Palace. However, there is a clear delineation between positivity and hope, and the differentiation goes far beyond semantics.

You demonstrate positivity, or optimism, if you think the future will be better than the present. Optimistic people tend to live on the sunny side of life. They see the glass as half-full and probably see life through beautifully colored lenses. They generally think that things will turn out just fine. Positivity, then, is an attitude. It doesn't concern itself with real information about the future and it may not have any specific goals. Some researchers call optimism an "illusion," or a "positive expectation bias." As such, positivity is partly based on temperament. Those who score higher on agreeableness and extroversion tend to be more optimistic by their very nature. Some babies come into the world inclined to embrace experience, while others shy away.

Hope, on the other hand, is the belief that the future will be better and that you have a role to play in making it so. You may be a hard-nosed realist or even a pessimist, someone who sees the world in a clear, cold light. Yet, hope compels you to take action to improve any situation that is important to you. It is not based on personality or disposition. Hope involves: (1) inspirational goal-setting; (2) sustained motivation to make progress toward accomplishing the goals; (3) having the flexibility to find new ways of getting to the goal when a particular pathway is blocked; and (4) having the ability to envision new goals when necessary. Hope, therefore, is far more than merely a positive mindset. Hope is a methodology used to build a better tomorrow. It isn't just wishful thinking. It's defining the work, leveraging the will and finding a way to pursue a preferred future. And hope deals with reality head-on.

Hope is a methodology used to build a better tomorrow.

The Stockdale Paradox

The Stockdale Paradox is a concept that was popularized by Jim Collins in his book *Good to Great*. It was named after James Stockdale, former vice-presidential candidate, naval officer and Vietnam prisoner of war. The main point of this paradox is that you must find a healthy balance between realism and optimism.

In a paradox, you find beneficial bits of wisdom. The difficulty is that when first hearing a paradox, it may sound confusing or counter-intuitive. It may even sound contradictory and may be hard to intuitively grasp. Such is the case with the paradoxical case of James Stockdale. At first glance, it may take some linguistic gymnastics to fully land it. But it poses a point that is well worth considering.

During the Vietnam War, Stockdale was held captive as a prisoner of war for over seven years. He was one of the highest-ranking naval officers taken hostage at the time. In the clutches of his captors, his life was made a living hell. During his horrific captivity, Stockdale was repeatedly tortured and had no reason to believe that he'd survive the conflict. Yet he found a way to stay alive by embracing the harshness of his situation with the buffering balance of hope.

*"You must never confuse faith that you will prevail in the end
– which you can never afford to lose – with the discipline to
confront the most brutal fact of your current reality,
whatever they might be."*

– STOCKDALE

According to Stockdale, "You must never confuse faith that you will prevail in the end – which you can never afford to lose – with the discipline to confront the most brutal fact of your current reality, whatever they might be." In the simplest explanation of this paradox, you must always have hope for the best in the future, while acknowledging realities and preparing for the worst. This paradoxical thinking has been one of the defining philosophies for great leaders making it through hardship and reaching their goals.

Whether it's surviving a torturous imprisonment in a POW camp or going through your own tribulations and trials, the Stockdale Paradox has merit to govern your thinking and behavior in trying times. The inherent contradictory dichotomy in the paradox holds a great lesson for how to achieve success and overcome formidable obstacles. It also flies in the face of unbridled optimism and positivity pushers who peddle sunshine without a plan.

In a discussion with Collins for his book, Stockdale spoke about how the optimists fared in camp. Here is Collins' recollection of that conversation:

"Who didn't make it out?"

"Oh, that's easy," he said. "The optimists."

"The optimists? I don't understand," I said, now completely confused, given what he'd said a hundred meters earlier.

"The optimists. Oh, they were the ones who said, 'We're going to be out by Christmas.' And Christmas would come, and Christmas would go. Then they'd say, 'We're going to be out by Easter.' And Easter would come, and Easter would go. And then Thanksgiving, and then it would be Christmas again. And they died of a broken heart."[42]

We all want circumstances to work out for our good. We want to be successful and happy. Reaching such a state will not come simply through positive visualization. Adopting an optimistic attitude may make you feel good for the moment, but all dreams must eventually devolve into hard work if you want to make any progress. No matter how many hot coals you walk across or how many pom poms you wave, advancement toward your goals will require more than a shift in mindset. Confronting the entire reality of your situation is instrumental for making gains. Better said, optimism is only half of hope. Positivity may provide you with an optimistic outlook on the future. Hope will give you the plan to get there, while dealing effectively with reality.

As for the application to business, hope helps leaders guard against the onslaught of disappointments that inevitably hit you in the real world of commerce. Optimism may drive innovation, but you must always keep your feet firmly planted on the plane of reality. Otherwise, leaders may find themselves stumbling blindly into situations that are insurmountable. Hope provides the optimism necessary to fuel passionate performance, the courage to face reality and the agility to assess any situation honestly and prepare for contingencies.

SIX

The Power of With

*Solitude, isolation, are painful things
and beyond human endurance.*

- JULES VERNE

On the main northeast ridge route to the top of Mount Everest lies a most unnerving landmark. For those adventurous enough to attempt to scale the summit, they will find the ghostly marker in a limestone alcove cave at 27,900 feet above sea level. *Green Boots* is the name given to the unidentified body of a climber who made the deadly mistake of getting separated from his party. Although the body has never been officially identified, it is believed to be the remains of Tsewang Paljor, an Indian climber who died on Everest in 1996. The term Green Boots originated from the green Koflach mountaineering boots on his feet.

On the tenth of May, 1996, Paljor and his party from the Indo-Tibetan Border Police expedition from India, were attempting to summit. As frequently happens in that frigid climate, they found themselves engulfed in a blinding blizzard. Several members of the team made the decision to turn back and descended to high camp. But Paljor and two others continued to climb. At around 15:45 Nepal Time, the three climbers radioed to their expedition leader that they had arrived at the top. On the summit, they meditated for a while and then left an offering of prayer flags and pitons.

One of the climbers decided to stay to spend extra time for religious ceremonies and instructed the other two to move down. They began their descent. The storm intensified. Radio contact was lost. And somehow so was their contact with one another. The three never made it back down to high camp. Green Boots joined the ranks of roughly 200 corpses remaining on Everest, all frozen in time. Their fatal mistake was choosing to separate from others in the midst of a storm.[43]

The Ethos of Lego

The Lego Group, maker of those ubiquitous brightly colored plastic construction toys, is a privately held company based in Billund, Denmark. The company's flagship product, interlocking plastic bricks, accompanied by an array of gears, figurines and various other parts, can be connected in countless ways to construct objects, including vehicles, buildings, space ships and working robots. They can be snapped together to create almost anything. In fact, according to Lego, six bricks of 2 x 4 studs can be combined in 915,103,765 different ways.[44] I'll take their word for it.

Lego pieces of all varieties constitute a universal system. Despite variation in the design and the purposes of individual pieces over the years, each piece remains compatible in some way with existing pieces. Each Lego piece is manufactured with precision to fit together with other pieces. When two pieces are engaged, they must fit firmly, yet be easily disassembled. Simply put, Lego blocks are designed to snap together. When they are connected, they can create almost anything the imagination can conjure up.

Just like Lego pieces, people are meant to *snap together*. Life is not a solo sport. Human beings are designed to connect in community. When we connect, we are capable of accomplishing some remarkable feats. The challenge comes in the fact that when facing adversity, many people tend to retreat from the very relationships that could potentially provide the support needed to weather the storm. Compounding the problem is the fact that in our society there is a growing trend toward individualism, independence and isolationism that could prove to be deadly.

Life is not a solo sport.
Human beings are designed to connect in community.
When we connect, we are capable of accomplishing
some remarkable feats.

With the coming of the information age, the pendulum has now swung to an emphasis on individualism. The playing field has been leveled by the sheer fact that all the information one could possibly need is only a few keystrokes away. If it were information alone that we needed, we really wouldn't need one another anymore. Life-sustaining information was once passed from one generation to the next. Such relational connectivity was once imperative for survival. Now we only need access to the internet to have our questions answered. We now have the knowledge of our forefathers at our fingertips. Likewise, we can gain access to information, conduct conference calls with team members globally, and produce webinars for clients without ever having to be face-to-face with anyone. Technology connects us to everyone and to no one.

We can claim hundreds, if not thousands, of friends on Facebook and yet be truly known to no one. We can be connected in gigantic networks, such as LinkedIn, and still lack for productive business relationships. We can have a flock of followers on Twitter and Instagram and never reveal anything personal or meaningful. It's the popularity parody. Technology has the ability to connect millions, while the million connections remain impersonal.

It is the phenomenon of this generation – people are widely socially connected, while remaining relationally isolated.

It is the phenomenon of this generation – people are widely socially connected, while remaining relationally isolated. Technology has bred a spirit of both independence and isolation. Independence in that we really don't need others to show us or teach us anything. We can get access to everything we desire to know all by ourselves. Access to information doesn't necessitate a teacher, coach, mentor, or even a parent to give us the information required to survive. Google allows us to explore every topic imaginable. YouTube entertains and shows us how to do things by watching a short video. Wikipedia provides collective intelligence. But none of them provide relational support.

The nature of interpersonal communication has changed dramatically as well. Families sit together at the dinner table in rapt silence, preoccupied on their smart devices – if they even still eat dinner together. Friends have multiple conversations simultaneously through texting and rarely hear each other's voices. Colleagues sit in tightly clustered cubicles, merely feet or floors apart, and prefer to type rather than talk to one another. Surrounded by a multitude of virtual friends, we find ourselves isolated from meaningful relationships. The art of small talk has been lost. And getting to know others deeply through conversation has been replaced by stalking on social media. Awash in a sea of humanity, we find ourselves swimming alone.

I don't want you to think that I'm trashing technology. Technology has produced advancements in science and society that previous generations never could have imagined. Technology is simply a tool. And, as a tool, it can be wielded for great good or abused to our own detriment. And one of the negative impacts of technology is that, left unchecked, it can actually impede our ability to relate to others in meaningful ways. We must master technology, or it will be our master. We must garner the discipline to disconnect occasionally from technology and reassemble ourselves to the life-giving nature of meaningful relationships.

The term "ethos" finds its origin in Greek and means custom, habit or character. In sociology it refers to the fundamental character or spirit of a culture; it's the underlying sentiment that informs the beliefs, customs, or practices of a group or society. While Lego blocks are indeed inanimate objects, they also have an ethos – or character – for they are constructed for a specific purpose. The ethos of Lego is connectivity. They are designed and manufactured to fit together to create fun. In fact, the name Lego comes from the Danish phrase *leg godt*, which means "play well."

Separated and isolated, they can easily become a nuisance, especially if found unexpectedly underfoot in the darkness. But when gathered and snapped together, they can be assembled to construct some of the most creative and captivating structures imaginable. In similar fashion, when we as human beings are connected in a collaborative way, we can be incredibly imaginative. When we come together, we can find the kind of support necessary to conquer our greatest challenges. Our collective intelligence makes us more creative. Teams provide both the encouragement and resources to accomplish great goals. And individuals need the emotional support provided within the context of community.

Loneliness Can Be Lethal

Imagine being confined to a small, dark room, with no contact with other people whatsoever for thirty days – voluntarily. Not many folks would jump at the chance for such extreme social isolation. But that's exactly the challenge that Rich Alati accepted in November of 2018. Alati, a professional US poker player, bet $100,000 that he could stay for a month in a small, completely dark room with nothing but a bed, a refrigerator and a bathroom. Even with all the resources he needed to survive, Alati broke down and couldn't make good on his bet. After twenty days, he negotiated his release and took a payout of $62,400. The isolation took its toll in more ways than merely minimizing his payout.

The negative effects of loneliness are numerous. Extreme isolation can be harmful to our minds and bodies. Alati was no exception. He reported having experienced a range of side effects including hallucinations, changes to his sleep cycle, disorientation and depression. But why is isolation so difficult for humans to withstand?

For starters, we are by nature social creatures. We are born into a social structure called the family. Here we grow and learn to interact with others. As we mature, we utilize the lessons learned in our nuclear family to build relationships outside the home and begin to create a sense of community with others. This network, when healthy, provides a sense of connectedness. In being connected with others, we receive emotional support and encouragement. The stronger those networks of support, the more we feel as if we belong. Without this sense of belonging, people can suffer from loneliness. This loneliness can lead to further isolation that can have a negative effect on a person's health.

Loneliness can be damaging to our emotional, mental and physical health. Socially isolated people are less able to deal with stressful situations. They are also likely to feel depressed and may have problems processing information. This can lead to difficulties with decision-making, as well as memory storage and recall. People who are lonely are also more susceptible to illness. Researchers have found that a lonely person's immune system responds differently to fighting viruses, making them more likely to develop illnesses.

The impact of social isolation increases when people are placed in physically isolated environments. For example, solitary confinement can have negative psychological effects on prisoners. These effects include significant increases in anxiety, panic attacks, increased levels of paranoia and loss of mental acuity. Many prisoners report long-term mental health challenges after being held in isolation.[45]

Clearly, we are social creatures. We depend upon regular contact with parents, siblings, spouses, friends and others for comfort, support and camaraderie. We all have a built-in need for love, acceptance, recognition and a sense of belonging. Yet, some people crave social contact more than others. Some of this disparity can be attributed to a difference in personality types. Extroverts crave contact with others. They are invigorated by social interaction. Introverts covet personal time, seldom feeling lonely when alone. But the distinction between aloneness and loneliness transcends typology, since even introverts can suffer the negative repercussions of loneliness.

Loneliness is deeply related to a *sense of self*. The less solid and stable this sense of self may be, the less connection there is to one's own true self, or *soul*. The less one is connected to their own true self, the more likely they are to suffer from the pain of loneliness. When someone feels empty inside, like a nobody or nonentity, the more likely they are to seek constant affirmation, attention and acceptance from others to validate their value and very existence. This most often occurs when someone has lost touch with their own feelings, thoughts and values. This usually results in low self-esteem, bad boundaries, anxiety and an inability to tolerate aloneness. In a way, you could say that a person with a disconnected sense of self is unconsciously missing and lonely for themselves. For such an individual, being alone is terrifying. They may actually fear disappearing if they are not validated by others.

On the other hand, the stronger the *sense of self*, the more aloneness one can tolerate and use productively. Solitude, if used effectively, can be an integral and indispensable part of the human experience. Time removed from others for thoughtful reflection and self-improvement can produce self-exploration, growth and individuation. It could be said that the capacity to accept and utilize some aloneness and solitude is a barometer of good mental health.[46]

Still, it is no coincidence that one of the worst tortures inflicted on human beings by others involves solitary confinement, ostracization, exile or excommunication. Excessive solitude is dangerous, even if self-imposed. Shunning of social contact can be induced by a number of factors including anger toward the world, uncertainty and anxiety, fear of intimacy or shame. For some, there is a tendency to pull away from social contact in the midst of chaos or crisis. Feelings of embarrassment or confusion may contribute to this tendency to want to hide from others. Not wanting to be a burden to others, they may not reach out for help when they need it. When this occurs, the result can be devastating. When someone self-quarantines from relationships, the very lifelines needed to provide emotional support are severed. Pulling away from others can produce a profound sense of alienation and disconnectedness.

According to Joel Salinas, "Emotional support and, in particular, having someone to listen are forms of social support that may independently help reduce the risk of stroke and dementia." Salinas is a researcher from Massachusetts General Hospital and Harvard Medical School. In one study, he and his team assessed the brain-derived neurotrophic factor (BDNF) levels in 3,383 participants from the Framingham Heart Study. In addition to increasing BDNF, greater social support also reduced the risk of early onset Alzheimer's and other issues related to brain health, including depression.[47]

*Seek to surround yourself with people who believe
the best in you, want the best for you
and expect the best from you.*

A big part of nurturing hope is found in being connected with others. As we have seen, hope involves the ability to set inspirational goals and to maintain high levels of energy in their pursuit. It also consists of believing that one has the power to impact the future in a positive way and the creativity to come up with alternative solutions when problems present themselves. But hope is also impacted greatly by choosing carefully to pursue goals *with* others who are supportive and encouraging. Hope is increased by creating a community of social support. Seek to surround yourself with people who believe the best in you, want the best for you and expect the best from you.

People with higher hope often have close connections with other people. They are interested in other people's goals and lives. High hope people also have an enhanced ability to embrace and assess the perspectives of others without threat. High hope is associated with more perceived social support, more social competence and less loneliness.

Life is not meant to be lived alone. This is particularly true when encountering life's adversities. When times are tough, resist the temptation to go it alone. Doing so can be deadly. Don't give in to the urge to withdraw relationally. Seek support from others. Find someone to listen, give counsel and encouragement. Get connected with a group of other folks who can provide the support necessary to weather a trying season.

Human beings are meant to live together within the nurturing structure of community. It's our interconnectedness that creates a web of support that can provide strength in the midst of our struggles. Tethered together, we can scale any mountain and survive even the most ferocious of storms. Isolated, we can easily find ourselves in a deadly predicament, disoriented and disconnected from the lifelines that are necessary to secure our safety.

We will never know exactly what sealed the fate of the three climbers from the Indo-Tibetan Border Police expedition. However, one thing is clear. They made the choice to separate themselves from the rest of their party and attempted to climb on their own. It was a fatal mistake. Green Boots lies alone in a limestone cave. His frozen remains serve as an eerie reminder of what can happen when you choose to climb alone.

SEVEN

Reverse Engineering Hope

It must be borne in mind that the tragedy of life
doesn't lie in not reaching your goal.
The tragedy lies in having no goals to reach.

- BENJAMIN E. MAYS

Reverse engineering is the process by which a man-made object is deconstructed to reveal its designs, architecture or composition. This is done with intent to extract knowledge or replicate the subject. When this process is applied to a natural phenomenon, we call it scientific research. This is the process that I have pursued in dissecting hope. Taking decades of scientific research, I have attempted to distill the salient points into language that can be understood easily and applied practically to build a brighter future for anyone. In spite of the fact that we're discussing the psychological phenomenon of hope, I think it appropriate to use the term reverse engineering. I do so because there are certain components of hope that must work together if there is to be a significant effect. I want to break hope down and discuss these moving parts individually. Then, I want to analyze how these elements function collectively to produce hope. And I want to show how, when these mechanisms are properly assembled, hope can be replicated.

As I mentioned earlier, it has often been said that, "Hope is not a strategy." I would whole-heartedly disagree. When these words are uttered, they are usually accompanied by a caution to not be passive or fall prey to mere wishful thinking. As we have seen, however, hope is very much an active proposition. It is a goal-directed disposition that is passionate about the pursuit of an established goal. Hope embraces reality and demonstrates the agility to assess progress, find alternate pathways and even reimagine goals when necessary. What I am trying to say is that hope is very much a strategy. In fact, it is the best strategy if you want to produce anything of value. Hope must be at the core of any worthwhile endeavor if those involved want it to be a successful pursuit. In fact, without hope to guide and inspire your efforts, they will be in vain.

With this understanding at the forefront of our discussion, let's turn our attention to the mechanisms of hope. Let's do some reverse engineering and look carefully at the various components of hope, with the intent of finding out which factors we can lean into to increase hope. There are essentially four elements that must be understood and leveraged to maximize hope. Let's break each one down to see how they apply to building a better tomorrow.

The Work — The Cerebral Side of Hope

Hope must have a goal. Without a clearly defined outcome, hope is reduced to a distant and indistinct dream. Without a goal, you have nothing more than a wish without substance. Hope is always goal-directed. The goal, in order to be fueled by hope, must be meaningful for those involved. A vision of the outcome must be sufficiently exhilarating to garner the energy necessary to pursue the vision with passion. The more inspirational the desired outcome, the more energy will be harnessed and utilized in its pursuit.

The *Work* of hope is the *cerebral side* of the equation. It is the *thinking* part that takes the theoretical and makes it practical. It establishes and clearly defines the outcome. The *Work* of hope is to set forth the overarching mission by painting a clear picture of a preferred future. The *Work*, therefore, is the *What* of hope. It is preceded by the brainstorming and white-boarding that must initiate any significant endeavor. Here, ideation is instrumental. Effective ideation involves seeking input from significant stakeholders. The more that stakeholders can own the process, the more effective the implementation.

A major mistake that is often made by leaders is to pontificate directives from on high. The fallacy in their thinking is that since they are the subject matter experts and because of their experience, they possess the knowledge and the wisdom necessary to set the course. There is a time and a place for strong and clear directives to be issued. However, a more directive style should be used sparingly and reserved for times when there is considerable disagreement or dissention in the ranks, which cannot be resolved. At such times, good leaders must make a call. And stand by it firmly.

In order for any idea to be executed with excellence,
each person involved in the process must emotionally
"own the outcome." It's not enough that people accept
or acquiesce to what is expected of them.
They need to fully adopt it as their own.

However, the vast majority of the time it is better for everyone involved to have a say in the outcome. Here is why. Suppose you are the leader and you have a great idea. When you bring it to the team, they lack the enthusiasm that you have about it. You believe strongly that it's the course that needs to be pursued, so you insist on having it your way and force everyone into compliance. You bulldoze your idea through the process to implementation. How well do you think your idea will be executed by those who lack buy-in and have little enthusiasm to pursue the process?

In order for any idea to be executed with excellence, each person involved in the process must emotionally "own the outcome." It's not enough that people accept or acquiesce to what is expected of them. They need to fully adopt it as their own. When you adopt a child, it's not a partial commitment. That child becomes your responsibility. You fully embrace that little one and commit your time, energy and resources to nurture him or her until they reach maturity. The same is true for any team endeavor. Each person must adopt the goal as their own if you want there to be exceptional execution. Everyone must have their fingerprints on the plan in order to emotionally buy-in and dedicate themselves wholeheartedly to its accomplishment. When everyone is emotionally vested in the product and process, then great things can happen. At that point, they are fully onboard. They both own the process and assume responsibility for the outcome.

So, hope always has a plan. Much has been set forth about how goals are best established. I will not attempt to parse out the process of goal-setting at this point. Suffice it to say, goals must be well-defined and clearly articulated. They must be time-bound, measurable and attainable. And, as we have said, they must be inspirational in order for those who are involved to personalize them.

Hope knows where it's going. Hope has a plan.
And the Work of hope is codifying that plan.

Thus, the *Work* of hope could be considered the systemic component. It takes the conceptual and morphs it into the overarching mission. It establishes the definition and direction of the endeavor. Without a clearly designated destination, one is left to merely wander. Hope knows where it's going. Hope has a plan. And the *Work* of hope is codifying that plan.

The Will — The Visceral Side of Hope

To accomplish anything of substance, one must possess both the skill and the will to make it happen. To have the skill means to possess the competencies necessary to get the work done. It's the talent to attain the goal. But completion of any task involves more than simply possessing the skillset to bring it to fruition. There is also an emotional element that fuels performance. This heartfelt investment in the outcome is what we call the *Will*. The *Will* is the visceral side of the equation. It's the heart to make it happen. It's the inspirational piece.

When someone possesses the *Will*, they rally the resources necessary to complete the project. These resources may be either internal or external. Internally, the *Will* may be the passion, motivation and emotional energy to stay in pursuit of the goal, even when challenges present themselves. The *Will* is the capacity to maintain enthusiasm in the face of hardship. Sometimes it is nothing more than the strength to take the next step – to put one foot in front of the other. It's the volition to keep moving toward the goal. Hope wills it to be done.

*The **Will** is the agency that creates momentum.*

Externally, hope involves rallying the people and resources necessary to take required action. Again, the more inspirational the goal and the more stakeholders own the endeavor, the more effective the execution. The *Will* is the fuel that produces the internal combustion to run the engine. It also engages the gears, which ultimately move the endeavor forward. The *Will* is the agency that creates momentum.

In challenging times this fuel level may run a bit low. When under stress, the gas guage on the dashboard can easily dip into the red. Dark clouds and rainy days can dampen one's spirits. This is when someone's emotional constitution is tested most. This is when guts and grit come into play. When the going gets tough, the *Will* engages a lower gear to make the steep ascent. The *Will* is the "never-quit-instinct" of hope that is necessary to keep climbing. The *Will* remains behind the wheel to keep the endeavor on course, even on winding and hilly roads.

The *Will* is an expression of the heart of the individual. It's a demonstration of a person's values. What is deemed of value will impact our thought processes, decision-making and performance. The *Will* is an expression of one's personal value construct. It is intrinsically what is most important to the individual. It shows what is personally vital for that person. And the more personal, the more impactful.

The *Will* is also the sustaining power in the pursuit of the goal. Since the *Will* involves mustering the internal and external resources necessary to ensure the success of the endeavor, it could be argued that it is the most important aspect of hope. While the *Work* establishes the definition and direction and the *Way* provides the tactical detail, nothing happens if there is no motivation to make it happen. Fueling the flames of the *Will* are crucial if any pursuit is to remain viable. Once the spirit is lost, no matter how glorious the goal may have been, it will be abandoned. Special care and attention must always be given to keeping this aspect of hope alive.

It could be said that the *Will* is the *Why* of hope. *Why* must always be the core. It is the very soul of the pursuit, because it's the reason. It is the essence of the endeavor. The *Why* is the driving force, providing fuel all the way to the finish. If there is a priority in terms of which component of hope is most critical, it would be the *Will* for it's vital to the life of any worthy pursuit. The *Will* is most closely aligned with purpose.

Later, we will explore ways in which we can more fully ignite the *Will*. There are a number of activities that can be used to fill the tank if the fuel level begins to run low. One can refuel by focusing on a few life-giving activities. Understanding certain principles and applying effective practices can renew the *Will*. Each of these will be explored in depth in a subsequent chapter. Suffice it to say, the *Will* is the fuel of the soul. It is imperative that it be monitored and maintained. When it is ignited, remarkable things can happen. A strong *Will* can leave an immense positive wake in the world.

The Way — The Tactical Side of Hope

When a goal is established, a direction must be set and a pathway chosen to move forward. The pathway is the means to get there. It involves identifying stakeholders, an accounting of resources needed and a timeline with measurable steps in the process. It is the *When*, the *Where* and the *How* of hope. The *Way* is the tactical side of hope.

The *Way* is also the *pivotal* part of hope. With every endeavor, there must be an anticipation of confronting obstacles along the way. They will most certainly come. When a chosen path is blocked, there must be an honest assessment of the cost required to remove, climb or circumvent the obstruction. When possible, modifications can be made to clear the hurdle and continue the pursuit. However, there are occasions when reality may dictate it's wiser to choose an alternate path. When this is the case, pathway thinking provides the agility and adaptability to alter course.

There are usually multiple routes that can be taken to arrive at a single destination. But, in order to take an alternate route, available resources need to be evaluated. To alter course, massive changes may be required. It takes courage to change horses in the middle of the stream. But failing to do so in a timely manner, when necessary, could mean that the entire endeavor drowns. This flexibility to alter course or unsaddle oneself from a faltering means or method is the creativity involved in Nexting.

Nexting is the concept of envisioning the next step. It is the continual process of predicting what is likely to happen based upon observable factors. This involves continual assessment of the situation, using pathway thinking to make modifications. An example of a company that failed in their Nexting capability was Blockbuster.

The last surviving Blockbuster Video store still stands and is open for business in Bend, Oregon. Like a fossil from a bygone era, the relic attracts fascination from those who remember a time when the presence of this behemoth once dominated the corporate landscape. In 2019, after the closure of locations in Alaska and Australia, the Oregon location officially became the World's Last Blockbuster on the planet. More of a novelty than a place to rent premiere videos, they hawk their own made-in-Oregon T-shirts, hoodies and foam trucker hats – all printed with the near-extinct chain's torn ticket logo boldly emblazoned across their merchandise. You can even purchase laminated replicas of its once popular membership cards, as well as bumper stickers that read, "I SURVIVED ALONG WITH THE LAST BLOCKBUSTER" in distressed capital letters.[48]

Once a thriving venue for video rentals, Blockbuster boasted over 9,000 outlets in the United States alone at its peak in the late '90s. With over 84,000 employees and 65 million registered customers, Blockbuster earned $800 million in late fees alone. Push fast-forward for one decade and Blockbuster was taken off life support, filing for bankruptcy with over $900 million in debt. So, what happened?

Blockbuster was founded by David Cook, a software supplier in the oil and gas industry. He realized that a well-franchised chain could grow to 1,500 units. And so, on October 19, 1985, he opened the first store in Dallas. They had an innovative barcode system, which gave the ability to track up to 10,000 VHS tapes per store to each registered customer. This meant that they could keep track of their inventory effectively and assess late fees.

In 1987, Blockbuster received an infusion of capital from a trio of investors, including Waste Management founder Wayne Huizenga, in return for voting control. After two months of intense disagreement, Cook left Blockbuster and Huizenga assumed control. Under Huizenga, Blockbuster embarked on an aggressive expansion plan, buying out existing video-rental chains and opening new stores at a rate of one per day. Just three years after the first store opened, Blockbuster was America's No. 1 video chain, with over 400 stores nationwide.

But as Blockbuster became a multibillion-dollar endeavor in the early '90s, Huizenga was worried about how emerging technology like cable television could hurt Blockbuster's video-store model. After briefly considering buying a cable company and developing plans to build a Blockbuster amusement park in Miami, he scrapped both and offloaded the entire enterprise to media giant Viacom for $8 billion in 1994. In the following two years, Blockbuster lost half its value.

Here was the problem. While Blockbuster and its new boss, John Antico, focused on brick-and-mortar stores, technological innovations were on the rise. In 1997, Reed Hastings founded Netflix, a DVD-by-mail rental service. Ironically, he did so partly out of frustration from having been assessed a forty dollar late fee from Blockbuster. Two years later, after having passed on the opportunity to buy Netflix for $50 million, Blockbuster teamed up with Enron to create their own video-on-demand service. However, it soon became clear to Enron that Blockbuster was too focused on their lucrative standing locations and had little time or commitment for the video-on-demand business. So, in 2001, Blockbuster walked away from the first major development of wide-scale movie streaming. Within a few years, Netflix and other competitors began to encroach upon Blockbuster's share of the market, not by undercutting them, but by reimagining video rental in the digital age. And the rest, as they say, is history.[49]

Blockbuster failed to accurately assess their market surroundings and to understand the necessity of Nexting. They failed to reimagine their services. They were so fixated on one method of delivery, that they were unable to unsaddle themselves from a tired horse. Consequently, they weren't able to ride off into a glorious sunset. Instead, their horse died in the desert. Deprived of imagination and healthy pathway thinking, the dream went into a coma and could not be resuscitated. Systems failed because they were singularly focused and unable to make a shift.

Whether professionally or personally, the ability to reimagine or re-goal is crucial. When one destination is clearly blocked or looks unlikely to provide through-passage, then courage steps in to set a new direction and establish an attainable goal. Such may be the case of someone facing terminal cancer. While the original goal may have been to fight off the rogue cellular invasion, the goal may need to be re-set if it becomes apparent that interventions are insufficient to ward off the mortal enemy. In such a case, the patient may choose instead to re-goal and commit to leaving a lasting legacy through philanthropy. They may choose, instead of opting for life-draining treatments, to spend quality time with friends and family. Or they may pursue spirituality and other endeavors that could bring comfort to the soul.

Re-goaling allows a person to abandon an unattainable goal,
while finding new meaning in another, more realistic goal.
Re-goaling is where hope meets courage.

Re-goaling is the act of recalibrating or reimagining one's goals. When one particular pathway is blocked, and the cost to overcome it is too great, setting a new course becomes necessary. Sometimes, the goal itself is pushed out of reach because of shifting circumstances. This is where re-goaling comes into play. Re-goaling allows a person to abandon an unattainable goal, while finding new meaning in another, more realistic goal. Re-goaling is where hope meets courage. Reimagining and recreating the *Way* can make every day meaningful and productive.

The With — The Relational Circle of Hope

Imagine the *Work*, the *Will* and the *Way* forming the three sides of a triangle. The *With*, then, encircles them all. It ties them all together in the context of community. The *With* refers to the people from whom you draw support in your endeavors. As we have said, humans are meant to live in community with others. There is great power in relational connectivity. Relationships can provide immense emotional support and encouragement. People and organizations tend to thrive in relationally rich environments. However, if not chosen wisely or abandoned, relationships (or the lack thereof) can lead to our own demise.

A simple way to state it is, when it comes to supporting our efforts, there are two kinds of people. There are balcony people and there are basement people. Balcony people are those who stand in the loft and applaud our performance. They challenge us to elevate our endeavors. They are the cheerleaders, who inspire us to bring our best game. They believe the best in us, want the best for us and expect the best from us. They fan the flame within us and, when necessary, light a fire underneath us. They offer encouragement and provide us with wise counsel. They call us to a higher level of living. Surround yourself with these people.

On the contrary, basement people dwell in the low places of life. They are often critical. They offer their own dark spin on just about everything. For them, there are a thousand reasons why things will never work out well. They are the dream-dashers and naysayers. They cast a negative pall over every sunny day. They leave a nasty wake in the world and drain you of your energy. They will throw you in the mud and then wallow around in it with you, for their misery loves your company. They have a unique capacity to kill your *Will*. They must be avoided at all cost. Draw strong boundaries and distance yourself from these folks, lest they rob you of the richness of your aspirations.

A word of caution at this point would be wise. Be careful not to confuse the realist with basement people. We all need folks in our lives who have a good read on reality. Even if the truth is not pleasant, it does not mean that those who shed an unfiltered light on the subject are necessarily negative. They may just be calling it as they see it. These realists should be embraced and their perspective appreciated. I have found many a realist to be wildly optimistic. They start their journey with a valid assessment of the situation, no matter how harsh that may be. But that doesn't mean that they can't envision an exhilarating end or that they're negative about the prospects. It just means that they don't deny the realities of the current conditions. These people are to be valued for their forthrightness. Be careful that you don't refuse to take their counsel into consideration.

Going it alone can be deadly. And selecting the wrong people to join you on your journey could easily put you in harm's way. Make sure that you select trustworthy people and stay securely tethered to their counsel, particularly when you find yourself in a blinding blizzard of swirling circumstances. Being tied together tightly to others who have your best interest at heart may be the very lifeline that keeps you from falling from the precipice into a deep crevasse. Surround yourself with those who will support you in your endeavors by sharpening and clarifying your *Work*, fanning your *Will* and providing counsel when it may be necessary to adjust your *Way*.

A Construct of Values

Axiology is a branch of philosophy that deals with values, as those of ethics, aesthetics, or religion. It's the study of what is valuable and how that which we value impacts our thought processes and decision-making. Axiology contributes significantly to motivational theory in that it postulates that our values are the driving force behind our thinking and our actions. It's both a powerful approach to motivational theory and highly predictive of behavior.

Robert Hartman is considered by many to be the modern father of axiology. According to his Value Theory, we all make decisions based upon how we view life as we look through three lenses. The *systemic lens* provides definition, dealing with the conceptual and the theoretical. This systemic lens is how we explain life. It's big picture thinking that ties all the elements of life together. It could be said that the systemic represents the *head*, or how we think things through. The *extrinsic lens* is how we do life. It is our understanding of work processes and work flow. It is the tactical side, or the *hands*, by which we make a difference by our doing. And then there is the *intrinsic lens* which could refer to the *heart*, or that which is deeply personal. The heart has to do with our relating, both to our feelings and in our friendships.

Hope could be considered a values construct. As we have seen by its mechanisms, there is the *Work*, the *Will* and the *Way* that comprise the construct of hope. There are parallels that can be drawn between this construct and the leading indicators of axiology, as defined by Hartman. The *Work* of hope can be compared to Hartman's Systemic dimension (head). The *Way* parallels the Extrinsic (hands). And the *Will* of hope can be compared to Value Theory's Intrinsic component (heart).

> *Hope springs from the heart,*
> *the hands and the head in various proportions.*

So, if I were to ask you to tell me where your hope springs from, would you be more inclined to say that it is found in your thinking, your feeling or in your doing? The reality is that hope springs from the heart, the hands and the head in various proportions, depending upon the individual. However, each of us has a propensity to lean more heavily in a certain direction.

If your hope is more founded in your thinking, then you are systemically grounded. If hope is more driven by your feelings, then you are intrinsically inclined. And, if hope finds its substance more in the doing, finding ways to attain your goals, then you may very well have a leaning toward the extrinsic. The point is that for hope to be sustained, it must have a solid footing in each of these arenas. They're each important. However, which ones we draw more upon will give insight into what we view as most important in our approach to life and living. The better the balance between these three dimensions of value, the more sustainable and powerful our hope will become.

How Are Your Heuristics?

Heuristics are the strategies that we employ in the decision-making process, derived from previous experiences with similar problems. We all make decisions in life based upon our intuitive capacity to perceive patterns. It's what Malcolm Gladwell calls "thin-slicing" in his popular book, *Blink*. As the subtitle suggests, it is the power of thinking without thinking. It is our ability to use limited information from the very narrow scope of personal experience to come to a conclusion.[50] When we say we have a gut reaction, a hunch or a feeling about something, then we are applying heuristics to draw a conclusion.

Such a conclusion is not entirely based upon empirical evidence or rationality, but rather upon our experience with patterns. This approach goes beyond data and reasoning and causes us to draw conclusions sometimes in spite of either. Heuristics could be seen as the intuitive judgment capacity that is developed through personal experience, training and knowledge. It is how the soul deals with uncertainty to make a decision that one can live with. The most common form of heuristics is trial and error.

Katherine Johnson was an African-American mathematician whose calculations of orbital mechanics were critical in the success of NASA's first and subsequent spaceflights. Being handpicked to be one of three black students to integrate West Virginia's graduate schools is something that many people may consider one of their life's most notable moments, but it's just one of several breakthroughs that marked Johnson's remarkable life. The highly acclaimed book and film *Hidden Figures* depicts the irony of her struggles for equality amidst the immense respect she garnered for her mathematical prowess and contributions to the space program. During her thirty-five year career with the program, she earned a reputation for mastering complex manual calculations and helped pioneer the use of computers that would later perform the same tasks. Johnson's work included calculating trajectories, launch windows and emergency return paths, ensuring that astronauts returned from their missions safely and were recovered quickly. In fact, her work was so valuable to the program that she was eventually awarded the Presidential Medal of Freedom and the Congressional Gold Medal.

On February 20, 1962, John Glenn flew the *Friendship 7* mission, becoming the first American to orbit the Earth. This mission was the first time that electronic computers were used to calculate the flight's orbit. Glenn, however, had officials call upon Johnson to verify the computer's numbers. Glenn asked for her specifically and refused to fly unless Johnson double-checked the calculations. His confidence in Johnson was based upon experience and personal knowledge of her professionalism. Glenn trusted her competence and her character. He chose to place his faith in her judgment over the data generated by computer calculations. His gut feeling about her contributed more to his comfort level than the facts spewed out by technology. His gut feeling is what we call heuristics.

How you make decisions is determined largely by how heavily you lean into your thoughts, feelings and actions. It also plays into how you generate hope. If your hope springs mostly from your head, then you will have a tendency to think your way to hope. Because you're cognitively inclined, it's easier for you to intellectually process the dynamics of difficulties. You come at life with a more philosophical approach. Because you tend to see things globally, you may not take them as personally. You can explain the good that could possibly come from challenges. You are rationally able to come up with reasons for the storm of circumstances and mentally maneuver yourself to a place where you can "wrap your head around" the problem. Having mentally parsed the problem, you can then come up with a solution. This solution will probably involve some form of redefining the situation.

At the same time, goal-setting is likely a strength of yours. You can take the theoretical and massage it into practical goals. You can mentally distill the mission into step-by-step plans. Painting a picture of a preferred future is the work of white-boarding. This, you likely do well. You thrive when given a chance to brainstorm ideas. You love to think challenges through and extrapolate circumstances to logical conclusions. You see interconnectivity in the details. You understand how one element can impact everything else and how the various parts work together as a whole. At the same time, you probably find fulfillment in projecting yourself into the future through your capacity for creative imagination.

If thinking is your strong suit, you must also embrace the relating and the doing sides of hope. It's one thing to understand a situation and entirely something different to act upon that knowledge. And just because you can intellectually justify something doesn't mean that you possess the emotional constitution necessary to fully engage in changing it. You may be proficient with the *Work* of thinking things through, but you will need to also balance the head with the hands and the heart of hope.

If, on the other hand, you find that hope springs from your emotions, then you are more intrinsically inclined. Hope for you is based upon your emotional fortitude and supportive friendships that fuel you through encouragement. It's important for you to find ways to fan the internal flames that keep hope burning bright. This may come through thoughtful reflection and introspection. For you, enthusiasm comes as you deal effectively with your internal conversations. You find great strength in your personal values. Possessing a deep sense of meaning and purpose is important to you. You don't just have a mission; you are on a mission. Leaning into your core values provides emotional equilibrium when circumstances could otherwise rock your world.

If you find yourself moving from the heart, it would serve you well to make a conscious attempt to come up with a solid plan. While you may have a fire in your belly, you may need help thinking through what practical steps you should take moving forward, or *Nexting*. Goal-setting may not be easy for you. Wholistic thinking and seeing how all the parts fit together may elude you. Seek counsel on putting together a plan of action. And, speaking of action, you will need to apply your emotional energy, exerting the effort to make progress. Get something started. It's not enough to feel it, you have to get active in the doing. And be prepared to be flexible, engaging healthy pathway thinking when needed. Embrace both the *Work* and the *Way* of hope. Combining these two with your powerful *Will* can propel you to higher levels of hope.

And lastly, you may find that you tend to lean into the extrinsic, or the *hands* side of hope. If this is the case, then you are adept at pathway thinking. It is easier for you to demonstrate agility in creating alternate pathways to reach the goal when one route is blocked. You thrive in the doing. You understand work process and work flow and you know what steps to take next. However, you may find yourself emotionally drained in the doing. It could also serve you well to spend more time thinking things through up front in order to avoid pitfalls. Because you would rather get going and make adjustments along the way, you may find yourself altering course more often than necessary, had you considered all of the possibilities before launching.

If this describes you, it may be helpful to set aside time for self-reflection in order to shore up your emotional side. Developing networks of relational support could also provide the encouragement and counsel to get you through tough times. It's not enough to have the determination to grind it out. Grit alone won't get you there. Make sure that your endeavors are solidly grounded in what is most important to you. Your activities must align with your core values. Make certain that you understand your *Why*. Good planning and monitoring your emotional energy will enhance your hope.

The *Work*, the *Will* and the *Way* form the three sides of the triangle of hope. While your triangle does not have to be equilateral to be effective, the more balanced these three dimensions, the better. And the better your balance, the better your heuristics or decision-making will become. When hope springs with force from all three, then hope can spring eternal. When encircled by healthy relationships, then hope becomes a formidable force to confront and conquer any challenge, no matter how insurmountable it may seem.

You Don't Have to Be an Engineer

I'm not mechanically inclined. I barely know how to change the oil in my car. I can assure you that I would have a hard time providing you with a coherent explanation of how an internal combustion engine operates. But that doesn't keep me from driving my car. I know how to put fuel in the tank, how to start the engine, and how to put it into gear to drive. That's really all I need to know to get from where I am to where I want to go.

Likewise, you don't have to understand the nuances of hope in order to leverage its power. If this chapter has been a bit overwhelming for you as we have attempted to reverse engineer hope, don't be discouraged. All you need to grasp is that hope is a matter of the *head*, the *hands* and the *heart*. You have to know where you are going *(Work)*, commit yourself to get behind the wheel to drive *(Way)* and be willing to find the fuel *(Will)* to sustain you on the journey. If you can do that, then hope is within your reach. Soon your problems will be in your rearview mirror.

Part Two Challenge

GO TO: **FIREPROOFHAPPINESS.COM**

COMPLETE THE HOPE RISES ASSESSMENT
USE COUPON CODE: FH20 FOR A 20% DISCOUNT

Part Three

PROGNOSIS: YOUR VIEW OF THE POSSIBILITIES

EIGHT

Making Life Better

Happiness is not the end of life; character is.

- HENRY WARD BEECHER

W hen I was a young boy, adults would occasionally ask me the question that adults are fond of asking children. What do you want to be when you grow up? My eyes would light up and my heart would skip a beat as I pondered the possibilities for my future. Literally, I would have a surge of excitement flow through my being because I knew at the ripe age of six exactly what I wanted to be when I grew up. Other kids may have wanted to pursue particular professions like becoming a doctor, or a fireman or a pro athlete. In my generation, becoming an astronaut filled many youthful imaginations with visions of one day walking on the moon. And a few even wanted to become the president. But none of those held any interest for me. My focus was clear and singular. I knew beyond any shadow of doubt that when I grew up, I was going to be Batman!

I had a glorious multifunctional protective suit (a pair of long pajamas) with the Batman crest on the chest. It was awesome. It had Velcro on the shoulders, where I would attach my cape before soaring around the house. My feats were legendary, at least within my own mind. I could jump from the couch to the recliner without touching the floor. And that was only the beginning. I was confident that when I grew up, I was going to fight evil. I was going to stand for justice. I was going to right all wrongs and change the world for good. And, when asked the question, a twinkle would come to my eyes and my lips would purse as I imagined the battles that I would soon fight to save the world.

All right, so I've always had a bit of a savior complex. But I still wake up each day with the enthusiasm of a child who believes he can make a significant difference in the world. And that's a good thing. I thrive helping leaders inspire their team members to bring their best to the table every day to accomplish something remarkable. I equip organizations with the tools and information needed to enhance their culture and engage their folks at a higher level. I serve as a catalyst for creativity, collaboration and productivity. I truly believe that in some small way I am changing the world for the better by offering hope.

*Most people are more focused on making a living
than they are on making a life.*

I think most folks fantasize, at one time or another, about being a super-hero. We all want to fight for right. We want to make a positive difference in the world. We want to know that our lives aren't being lived in vain. Unfortunately, I believe that most people are frustrated because they don't feel as if they're making a difference. Many feel as though they are trapped in a hamster cage, running incessantly on a wheel to get a piece of cheese that seems just out of reach. When asked what they do, you rarely see a twinkle come to their eyes as they describe their endeavors. This is likely due to the fact that most people are more focused on making a living than they are on making a life.

Far too many folks measure life by what they do, what they drive or what they are in debt to acquire. Society tends to measure personal worth in terms of titles, toys and trinkets of success. As a whole, the world places more emphasis on doing rather than on being. Which, of course, is the exact opposite of what truly brings meaning to life. Life flows from being, not doing.

Life flows from being, not doing.

Let me explain. If you tied apples onto a willow tree, would it then become an apple tree? Of course not. Regardless of how you may fill its branches with fruit, it still remains a willow. Eventually, the fruit will rot and fall to the ground and the truth will be glaringly self-evident. However, if you plant an apple tree, tenderly nurture it and allow nature to run its course, then you don't have to worry about what kind of fruit it will bear. An apple tree, if healthy, will always produce apples. You don't have to go through any artificial gyrations. You just have to wait and it will produce. Bearing apples is the natural result of being an apple tree. Bearing flows from being. Or, said differently, doing should always flow from being. Doing doesn't necessarily define being.

It's odd to me the gyrations people will sometimes go through to prove that they can bear fruit of a desired nature. Even when all of nature itself will tell you otherwise, there are those among us who "tie on the trappings" that they believe will bring meaning and happiness to life. They try to convince themselves and others that their fruit, though artificial, is still sweet. But, in spite of their efforts, life remains empty and unfulfilling.

Earlier in my career, I served as the leader of a high-energy, fast-growing non-profit organization that did much good in our community. A high-profile individual joined our ranks who floated in some pretty lofty circles. He was seemingly an astute businessman and a well-known philanthropist who possessed many talents. One of those talents was the ability to garner attention by letting it be known just how well-connected he was and how much he had contributed to a number of worthy causes. Many were convinced that he was a wonderful person to have supporting our cause. But I had concerns. Although I have to confess, he was pretty impressive. Nevertheless, I was cautious.

But truth is always borne out over time. The fruit began to rot. And it began to drop and stink. His promises turned out to be hollow. His connections were tenuous at best. It turned out that he was nothing more than a common conman, a shyster behind an extensive Ponzi scheme. He was a fraud. He simply moved the shells around, using sleight-of-hand to distract attention away from his deficit in character. The fruit wasn't real. It was "tied on." His doing, in the end, was not a reflection of his being. His being was rotten and the fruit it produced was rancid. What once passed as good deeds were actually manufactured at the expense of the unwitting. It was fake fruit.

Character vs. Competencies

Competencies are a central focus for many organizations. We hire for competence. We help people grow in their competencies and we measure competencies to mark progress. I'm not saying that there is anything wrong with this approach. In fact, it's necessary. People must possess the skills necessary to do their jobs effectively. But competencies are about what someone can do. It doesn't necessarily speak to the core of who they are or their long-term capacity for productivity. In other words, competencies are non-predictive of future success.

The nature of the tree will determine the nature of the fruit.
Character defines the true nature of the tree.

Character, on the other hand, is about being. Character defines who one is constitutionally. If someone is constitutionally good, then good things will flow from their being. If someone is constitutionally kind, then kindness will flow from their being. And it will happen naturally and consistently. It will not be forced or fabricated. It will be true fruit. Because the nature of the tree will determine the nature of the fruit. Character defines the true nature of the tree.

But character is harder to measure than competency. It takes longer to assess. We don't always have or take the time to wait to see what fruit the tree will bear. So, we rush to judgment by measuring competency. But our assessment of competencies will always have shortcomings. The world and the marketplace are filled with highly capable and competent conmen and women, who through their power of persuasion and well-cultivated impressions make us believe that their fruit is sweet. We all, to one degree or another, can fall prey to the propensity to pretend to be something other than what we truly are.

I have, more often than I care to admit, tried to leave an impression that I was something more than I actually knew I was. Maybe it was a little white lie, a slight exaggeration, a spin on a story or an outright untruth for the sake of posturing. In the moment, I slipped into the temptation to create an image of myself that was a bit more robust than reality. But when I walked away, it felt hollow. I knew better, so why was I trying to impress? Did I feel that the truth wasn't enough? Was I trying to measure up to some fictitious standard? Or maybe I had simply been sucked into the false narrative that is propagated by society. You know those messages that ring in your head like, "Go big or go home!" "Be bold to be heard!" "Dress to impress." "Fake it 'till you make it!"

So, we "tie on" the trappings necessary to float effectively in our social circles, paying more attention to what we and others "do," all the while losing sight of our being. And we fall victim to the fatal fallacy that says fake fruit will bring fulfillment. In so doing, we may gain the temporary approval of the world. But we lose our very souls.

Tumultuous times often wash away all the trappings. Calamity can leave us exposed for who we really are. We can be left bare and vulnerable. In a crisis, character becomes clear. One of the benefits of challenging times is that we have to actually face who we really are. All of a sudden, our being becomes more important than our doing. This stark revelation profoundly frames a healthy view of goal-setting.

> *Tumultuous times often wash away all the trappings.*
> *Calamity can leave us exposed for who we really are.*

What's the Goal?

Let me back up for a moment and try to offer another perspective on this idea of doing versus being that may provide more clarity. We all are very familiar with goal-setting. Whether personally or professionally, we set goals. They may come in the form of New Year's resolutions or a five-year growth plan for the business. Either way, goals are the sights we set on what we plan to do or accomplish. We are told that, in order to be effective, they should be specific, measurable, achievable, relevant and time-bound. So, we make our list and we set out to make them happen. But goal-setting and the actions necessary to accomplish those goals will not necessarily mean that the results will be long-lasting or sustainable if our underlying values do not shift. Let me explain.

> Our **doing** can easily be compromised when there hasn't been a shift in our values. If our efforts are entirely focused on the **doing**, then core beliefs have not been properly addressed. We need to focus on the hard work of shifting our **being**.

Let's suppose that you set a personal goal to lose ten pounds. That's a common resolution. What would you have to do to lose the unwanted weight? We all know that you would have to watch what you eat, exercise, hydrate well and get good rest. So, let's say that for two weeks you do all of those things and you begin to see progress. You drop three pounds. You are elated. Then, on Friday night, you go to your favorite buffet with the family. At that point you might say something to yourself like, "I've been extremely good sticking to my weight loss program. Tonight, I am going to reward myself." So, what do you do? You go back for seconds, of course. And then dessert. After all, you deserve it, right?

Or perhaps you work the plan for months and finally reach your goal weight. Then to celebrate, you indulge yourself with pizza and beer. Such "rewards" are actually self-defeating behaviors that thwart our progress. Our *doing* can easily be compromised when there hasn't been a shift in our values. If our efforts are entirely focused on the *doing*, then core beliefs have not been properly addressed. We need to focus on the hard work of shifting our *being*. Rather than placing the emphasis on *doing* certain behaviors simply to garner a desired result, we should instead concentrate on changing from the core of our *being*.

Suppose for a moment that you were actually able to shift your focus to *being* a different kind of person. Instead of *doing* certain behaviors to get a result, you began to focus on shifting your values. Instead of simply setting a goal to lose ten pounds, what if you concentrated on *being* a healthy person? How would that shift in values change your thought processes and decisions? Think about the choices that a healthy person would make. Among many other behaviors, a healthy person would eat well, exercise regularly, hydrate adequately and get plenty of rest. At first glance, the doing may look very similar to the list made by goal-setting. But the motivation is entirely different and the results would be sustainable. A healthy person, in essence, would tend to make healthy choices. A good and healthy tree bears good fruit – consistently.

When your value construct changes, so does your life.
Character growth involves shifting one's value construct
in a positive and permanent way.

Now suppose someone who is committed to *being* a healthy person goes to the same buffet on Friday night with the family. What kind of choices does a healthy person make? And, when a healthy person loses the ten pounds, they celebrate without self-sabotaging. They continue to make healthy choices. Maybe not all the time. Maybe not perfectly. But *their being* is much more likely to drive their *doing*. It's natural and effective.

It's true fruit. When your value construct changes, so does your life. Character growth involves shifting one's value construct in a positive and permanent way.

Making Life Better

Making life better involves being better at life. Maybe the greatest benefit of walking through fire is the fact that we have the opportunity for our character to be refined. But the path to character refinement is not an easy journey. It certainly isn't for the faint of heart. I can't offer you seven simple steps to a better life. It requires far more soul-searching and reflection. It requires vulnerability. It requires humility. However, if we stay committed to do the hard work necessary to strengthen the core of our being, the fruit will ultimately be sweeter. We will bring true fruit to life, love and work. Sometimes, the very things you want to remove from your life are the very things that life can use to help you improve. A challenge can be life's chisel, chipping away at the rough edges of our character.

Making life better involves being better at life.

In 2002, when I was forty-two years old, I was forced to make an unexpected vocational transition. I was relieved of my duties as the leader of a thriving non-profit organization. To put it bluntly, I was fired. Not because of anything of my doing. I had done nothing inappropriate. And I certainly wasn't incompetent. Rather, a series of curious extenuating circumstances left the board of directors bewildered. The details aren't important to my point, but I can tell you that it was an excruciatingly painful chapter of my life story. I felt betrayed. I felt abandoned. I felt that I had been unfairly dismissed and I was embarrassed. I had led and built the organization from its inception into a thriving, high-impact enterprise that was truly making a difference in the lives of many throughout our community. It was my dream job. And then it was gone. It was tough.

Lest you think that I am playing the victim card, there is much that I would have done differently if I had the chance to do it over. I spent quite a few hours with counselors and coaches dissecting the cadaver and assessing what I could have changed if given the chance. I learned and grew through the process. But the pain and stress at the time were almost unbearable. Almost overnight, I found myself a single parent of two pre-teens. And, thanks to a beleaguered board, I was also unemployed, with a highly specialized set of skills and no other job prospects on the horizon.

I wish I could tell you that the transition was easy, but it wasn't. In fact, for a number of months I had a hard time envisioning any future at all. Fortunately, I had a strong network of support. From my relational sphere, I received immense encouragement, counsel and emotional support. Their investment of time and energy eventually gave me the strength to begin to dream new dreams. I began to explore the possibilities.

Several months later, a financial group in the mortgage space discovered that I was available. The president of their Florida operations reached out to explore my interest in joining their team as the Chief People Officer for the state. I was ecstatic about the possibility of heading up the Human Resources Department of this dynamic burgeoning group, whose core values were so closely aligned with my own. However, before the offer could be culminated, word came down from corporate that the position was redundant. There was already a Chief People Officer at their home office in Atlanta and there would not be a second one in Florida. If I still wanted to come aboard, I would have to go through extensive training to become a loan officer and originate in the field for at least a year to learn the industry. Then, I could explore other possibilities within the organization, if I wanted to do so. It wasn't what I had envisioned for myself at forty-two. I would essentially be starting over from the ground up in an unfamiliar industry.

I was at a crossroads. I had no background in financial services. I didn't have a clue about loan originations. It wasn't something that I was honestly interested in doing at the time. But the offer was before me and I didn't have many other options to consider. So, I made a decision to reinvent myself. I took on the challenge. I would learn an industry I knew relatively little about and I would do so because my children and I needed it. It wasn't my preferred path but it was the path before me. I made a decision to pursue it wholeheartedly. I threw myself into the training and graduated near the top of my class. I hit the field with the enthusiasm of a recent college graduate. After my first eleven months of helping people "fulfill the dream of home ownership," I was in the running for Rookie of the Year in our company and was among the Top Rookie Originators in the country. But before I tout my praises too highly, let me remind you that just a few short years later, the housing market crashed. Probably, in no small part, due to placing people like me in roles like that. I'm just saying!

But here is the rest of the story. After originating loans in Florida for a year, I moved to the corporate offices in Atlanta. By then, I had remarried and moving to Atlanta gave us an opportunity to be closer to my new bride's aging parents. The organization created a VP role for me in the Recruiting Department. There, my team and I had the opportunity to create programs for our strategic partners that kept our funnel of candidates filled with prospects, brought new loans to our officers and became a windfall for the organization. It was a win on all fronts. And it was an exhilarating ride.

In 2006, just before the housing market crashed, I reinvented myself again by assuming the role of Chief People Officer for a group in the automotive space. That run was short-lived, as I made the brilliant decision to hang out my own shingle and start my own consulting business in January of 2008. I couldn't have chosen a worse time to launch a new endeavor. Attempting to build a solo business, timed with the start of the Great Recession, was an adventure of a lifetime (I say that tongue-in-cheek). The only thing that kept me going during those early days was a vision of what I believed could be and the agility to try multiple paths. When one path became impassable, I diverted to another. When the horse that I was riding couldn't cross the stream, I changed to another. When the projects I was working on faltered, I thought up fresh ones. The only thing I knew for sure was that tomorrow was going to be better than today. Quite frankly, it had to be. I believed in what I was doing. And, fortunately, my wife believed in me too. We had hope.

Sometimes, the very things you want to remove from your life are the very things that life can use to help you improve.

That was several years ago now. And I am thrilled to tell you that I am still putting food on the table and loving life. I can honestly say that I could never have dreamt that my life would run this course. I could never have envisioned it. I can also tell you that I wouldn't trade a single minute of it for anything different. I have the confidence of knowing that I can weather even the most severe of storms. I've been there and done it. I've had to reimagine life and work. I've had to start over. I've had to re-goal. I know it can be done. It's hard. It's stressful. It's, at times, overwhelming. But that's what makes life the great adventure. Embrace the unexpected.

Sometimes, the very things you want to remove from your life are the very things that life can use to help you improve. The fiery trials of life can serve to refine your metal. And adversity can become the anvil upon which your life is forged. Challenges can grind off the rough edges and smooth out your character. Allow the process to temper you until your being is sharp.

None of this is to say that goal-setting is not important. It is. But maybe what we become is more important than what we do. With hope as your guide, you can look a little deeper and do the hard work of cultivating your character. When you do, you will have sweet fruit to savor no matter what season of life you may be in.

Be Batman

Have you ever wondered why adults ask kids what they want to be when they grow up? I have my own theory. I think that most adults are so disillusioned, so disenfranchised and discouraged about the trajectory of their lives and work that they ask that question of kids in the hope of getting fresh ideas for a new career path!

You will find a better life
by becoming better at life.

The truth is, if you make your focus to *be better*, then I assure you that you will experience a cataclysmic shift that will rock your world for the good. Doing so will require you to take a long, deep look within. You may have to reassess your values. You will most certainly have to humble yourself and admit that you have been wrong in some of your thinking. But, if you hang in there, you might very well wind up with a different perspective. Your clarity and compassion may increase. Your self-understanding and purpose may come into focus. You may learn how to become your best self. You will find a better life by becoming better at life. And better at love and work too. And you will build your best life by becoming your best self.

One of the most profound statements a person can make is, "I enjoy being myself." A statement like that carries courage and confidence that not everyone possesses. When you can look yourself in the mirror and feel good about who you are becoming, then your world becomes a brighter place. Being able to say that isn't based upon perfection or accomplishments, but rather a commitment to growth and health. It means being thorough in addressing the most important issues of character development. It involves building a value construct that serves as a foundation for continual improvement. It is all about building from the core of your being and bearing good fruit.

Be the best you that you can be.
Don't be a second-rate knock-off of someone else. BE YOU!
In reality, it's the only thing you can be –
because everyone else is taken.

Since my children were young, I have encouraged them to be their best selves. While it can be helpful to look to others for inspiration, I never wanted them to try and be anyone but themselves. To that end I have often said, "Be the best you that you can be. Don't be a second-rate knock-off of someone else. BE YOU! In reality, it's the only thing you can be – because everyone else is taken."

Hardships and setbacks force us to grow in areas that we may have previously resisted. Growth requires you to focus on being the best you that you can be. It demands that you re-create yourself – for the better – continuously. Always be your best self. That is, unless you can be Batman. If you can, then always be Batman!

NINE

Keep Calm and Carry On

The essence of philosophy is that a man should so live that his happiness shall depend as little as possible on external things.

- EPICTETUS

You've likely seen it at one time or another. Emblazoned on a bright red background is the white image of an imperial crown. Underneath, in bold capital letters it simply says, "KEEP CALM AND CARRY ON." This was the message on a motivational poster produced by the British government in 1939 in preparation for World War II. The poster was intended to raise the morale of the British public as they faced imminent air strikes on major cities. But, in spite of its current popularity, it was rarely seen posted in public throughout the war. Although 2.5 million copies were printed, and although the blitz did become a reality, the poster was little known until a copy was rediscovered in 2000 at Barter Books, a bookshop in Alnwick, England.[51]

When times are tough, mottos and slogans
do little to emotionally engage the masses.
What people really need is hope.

The poster was designed by the Ministry of Information in the summer of 1939. It was produced as part of a series of three "Home Publicity" posters. Each morale boosting slogan was under the representation of a Tudor Crown, the symbol of the state. They were intended to increase British resolve in the event of wartime disaster. Although a massive number were printed, they were never sanctioned for public display. Instead, the copies remained in cold storage. In October of 1939 the Ministry of Information canceled its publicity campaign following criticism of its cost and impact. Many people claimed not to have seen the posters, while those who did regarded them as patronizing and divisive. The campaign to boost morale was a resounding failure. In April 1940, they were pulped as part of the Paper Salvage campaign.[52]

Perhaps the point is that posters and platitudes are insufficient to boost morale when facing wartime disasters. When times are tough, mottos and slogans do little to emotionally engage the masses. What people really need is hope.

Your Peacetime Plan Won't Work in War

It's somewhat fun and fairly easy to create imaginative plans when times are good. When you have both the resources and the personnel, putting together a brilliant strategy is somewhat simple. But everything can change in a heartbeat once the first explosion goes off. When you find yourself in the foxhole taking on fire, the landscape can suddenly look drastically different.

Facing adversity can thwart the best of plans. Blocked pathways can be discouraging. Limited resources can make things rough. Stress from changing circumstances can be unsettling. Uncertainty can shake you to the very core. This uncertainty can produce worries that surface in the form of what if questions. Questions like: "What if I get quarantined and can't work?" or "What if we lose those clients?" or even, "What if I lose my job?" Of course, these are all rhetorical questions. Nevertheless, they can bombard our brains and paralyze us in fear. If we aren't careful, we can find ourselves frozen in the foxhole, rendered incapable of combatting the true enemy – our own sense of helplessness.

Depression simply defined is the absence of hope.
When hope is lost, the soul sinks.

Helplessness and hopelessness can be devastating. Depression simply defined is the absence of hope. When hope is lost, the soul sinks. It takes courage and a deep sense of calling to combat these mental invaders. As we have discussed earlier, hope serves as a buffer against hopelessness. While the two may co-exist, the greater the presence of the resilience factor of hope, the more it offsets the risk factor of hopelessness.

*Even if your efforts do not change the external circumstances,
your choices can still have a powerful impact on what happens
internally. You may not be able to control the outcome,
but you can always control you.*

Helplessness is the feeling that no matter what you do, your actions won't make a difference in the outcome. This is never the case. Even if your efforts do not change the external circumstances, your choices can still have a powerful impact on what happens internally. You may not be able to control the outcome, but you can always control you. As we have seen, one of the greatest outcomes of hardship may very well be the refinement of our character. In other words, without you and your efforts, nothing positive will ever happen within you. With every choice, you are constructing your character. So, take advantage of the opportunity and never waste a crisis, no matter how dire the circumstances.

Viktor Frankl was an Austrian neurologist and psychiatrist who survived four Nazi concentration camps and lived to write about it. Imprisoned and conscripted by the SS to document their experiments, he was witness to some of the most appalling atrocities that mankind has ever perpetrated against his own in all of human history. Yet, in the midst of such depravity and calamity, he caught glimpses of the irrepressible goodness of the human spirit shown in self-giving acts of courage. In his classic work, *Man's Search for Meaning*, Frankl offers profound insights on the nature of man and the importance of having a hopeful focus on the future in the midst of tragedy. He writes:

> "It is a peculiarity of man that he can only live by looking to the future. And this is his salvation in the most difficult moments of his existence, although he sometimes has to force his mind to the task."

"A man who let himself decline because he could not see any future goal found himself occupied with retrospective thoughts. In a different connection, we have already spoken of the tendency there was to look into the past, to help make the present, with all its horrors, less real. But in robbing the present of its reality there lay a certain danger. It became easy to overlook the opportunities to make something positive of camp life, opportunities which really did exist. Regarding our 'provisional existence' as unreal was in itself an important factor in causing the prisoners to lose their hold on life; everything in a way became pointless. Such people forgot that often it is just such an exceptionally difficult external situation which give man the opportunity to grow spiritually beyond himself. Instead of taking the camp's difficulties as a test of their inner strength, they did not take their life seriously and despised it as something of no consequence. They preferred to close their eyes and to live in the past. Life for such people became meaningless."

"The prisoner who had lost faith in the future – his future – was doomed. With his loss of belief in the future, he also lost his spiritual hold; he let himself decline and become subject to mental and physical decay. Usually this happened quite suddenly, in the form of a crisis, the symptoms of which were familiar to the experienced camp inmate. We all feared this moment – not for ourselves, which would have been pointless, but for our friends. Usually it began with the prisoner refusing one morning to get dressed and wash or to go out on the parade grounds. No entreaties, no blows, no threats had any effect. He just lay there, hardly moving. If this crisis was brought about by an illness, he refused to be taken to the sickbay or to do anything to help himself. He simply gave up. There he remained, lying in his own excreta, and nothing bothered him anymore."

"Those who know how close the connection is between the state of mind of a man – his courage and hope, or lack of them – and the state of immunity of his body will understand that the sudden loss of hope and courage can have a deadly effect."[53]

For Frankl, faith in the future – or hope – and the will to live were inextricably intertwined. From his perspective, the greatest human triumph is achieved by the defiant human spirit, even when stripped to its naked existence and confronted with horrific tragedy. Hope explains how courage can be cultivated in the midst of great adversities.

Simple positivity is insufficient as a sustaining concept in the face of the harsh realities of human suffering.

In contrast, simple positivity is insufficient as a sustaining concept in the face of the harsh realities of human suffering. In essence, existing models of optimism are primarily based upon a confidence in one's own competence and the expectation of positive outcomes. These models contribute to effective coping, success, and well-being among healthy functioning individuals in affluent and individualistic societies. This is true because the main emphasis in these environments is on developing personal mastery over one's destiny and the pursuit of personal success. This focus on the self clearly reflects an American can-do-attitude, but does not work as well in places less fortunate. While there are great benefits in possessing a positive explanatory style of life events and a general bright expectation of the future, it comes up inadequate to explain inescapable suffering or provide a pathway to proceed that comes through hope.

To link expectations of positive outcomes entirely to one's own abilities severely restricts the wide range of sources of hope available. Hope may be found in circles of support, spiritual growth, inner transformation and finding deeper meaning in life in the midst of suffering. Suffice it to say, plans made in times or peace and prosperity will not work in times or war. Hope exercises the courage to prepare for psychological warfare.

Preparing for War

It took the horror of Nazi death camps for Viktor Frankl to come to an understanding of what he would later refer to as tragic optimism. He defined tragic optimism as "an optimism in the face of tragedy ... addressing present day concerns and how it is possible to 'say yes to life' in spite of all the tragic aspects of human existence. To hark back to its title, it is hoped that an 'optimism' for our future may flow from the lessons learned from our 'tragic' past."[54] Frankl's understanding of tragic optimism is the essence of what I am calling hope.

After surviving the Holocaust, Frankl wrote *Man's Search for Meaning*, discussing the critical nature of one's attitude toward suffering. He was not willing to engage in what he called false illusions or artificial optimism. He embraced hope, a faith in the future, as a posture to be adopted in the face of terror and tragedy. He taught that whatever sufferings we may endure and however oppressive and grim the situation may be, we can always choose the stance we take toward our suffering.

He demonstrated a greater dimension of hope; namely, that no matter the horrific atrocities one may be forced to face, and no manner of dehumanizing deprivation and degradation one may imagine, can strip someone of his human dignity involuntarily. No matter the pains inflicted upon him by his captors, Frankl held firmly to his abiding hope in the meaning and values of life. His defiant spirit and courage in the most hopeless, helpless situations bear witness to the power of hope. It would serve us well to understand hope, as Frankl describes it, in terms of tragic optimism.

Based upon Frankl's writings, we can identify five essential components that comprise tragic optimism (hope). Defining and understanding these will help us fight a better battle against negative influences that would assault our joy in life. Applying these principles, we can begin to construct a psychological bunker to protect us from emotional bombardment, brought about by destructive circumstances. And ultimately, we can win the war that is constantly being waged over our spirit, at the threshold of our mind.

1. **Accept what cannot be changed.**

    Acceptance of reality is an important defining characteristic of hope. This essential element of hope separates itself from other models of optimism in that it confronts and embraces reality, no matter how painful and gloomy it may be. Unless and until someone accepts the dark side of life and an honest assessment of grim reality, without delusion or denial, one cannot discover hope. The exploration of new pathways is only made possible when one assumes a proper posture toward reality.

A strong grasp on reality is the hallmark of mental health.

It's one of the most widely held assumptions that a strong grasp on reality is the hallmark of mental health. Enduring hope must be based upon a realistic assessment of factors at play, no matter how pessimistic the prospect. Such realism does not preclude the presence of positive beliefs and attitudes anchored to personal values. Quite the contrary, it makes their contrast more impactful, standing out against the dark background of circumstances.

This sense of acceptance is stated well in the Serenity Prayer, credited to the late American theologian Reinhold Niebuhr. It says, "God, grant me the serenity to accept the things I cannot change, courage to change the things I can, and wisdom to know the difference."[55] Accepting the harsh realities of life and boldly facing the world with all its evils is the pathway to achieving serenity and rebuilding a shattered life.

When false optimism eventually gives way to realistic pessimism, one is faced with a choice – either fade away in depression or embrace hope. Acceptance involves a double affirmation. Say *yes* to suffering and death. And say *yes* to meaning and life. Interestingly enough, suffering intensifies hope when there is acceptance coupled with affirmation. Suffering doesn't define us, unless we allow it to do so. Our lives should define suffering by asking, "What will we now make of this?"

Affirmation of the value and meaning of life
is the first positive step toward dealing with traumas
and rebuilding shattered assumptions.

2. **Affirm the inherent meaning and value of life.**

Affirmation of the value and meaning of life is the first positive step toward dealing with traumas and rebuilding shattered assumptions. Affirmation is simply the celebration of life and being alive. Life is full of meaning in and of itself. Life is inherently valuable and it's good to be alive.

The affirmation of life is the cornerstone of hope. Without a firm belief that meaning can be found in all aspects of life, including tragedy, it would be difficult to experience peace in the face of adversities. Hope is meaning-oriented and value-based. It's based upon a deeply cherished set of core values, giving meaning to life. These values may include achievement, intimacy, self-acceptance, self-transcendence and spirituality. Hope is unshakable to the extent that these personal values and meaning are deeply and securely held.

As an example, Frankl would quite frequently have vivid internal conversations with his wife, Elsa, although she was imprisoned elsewhere and not present. His deep abiding love for his wife and his intimate, internal dialogues with her endowed his existence with meaning and hope. He concluded: "Love goes very far beyond the physical person of the beloved. It finds its deepest meaning in his spiritual being, his inner self."[56]

Achievement, or the hope of future achievement, was another major source of meaning for Frankl as he languished in the death camps. He greatly valued his unfinished manuscript espousing logotherapy. Envisioning himself giving public lectures sometime in the future enabled him to transcend the hopelessness of his oppressive situation. He held specific visions of future events and that kept his spirits elevated.

For Frankl, "meaning in life enables us to make sense of our existence despite guilt, suffering, injustice and the inevitability of life."[57] Therefore, we must find something worth living and dying for, if we are to survive in life. We know how to endure and survive, once we know why we exist. Frankl, himself, would reflect, "As we said before, any attempt to restore a man's inner strength in the camp had first to succeed in showing him some future goal. Nietzsche's words, 'He who has a why to live for can bear with almost any how,' could be the guiding motto for all psychotherapeutic and psychohygienic efforts regarding prisoners."[58]

Self-transcendence is shifting the focus from self to serving others. In doing so, one may feel as if he is serving a higher purpose than simply self-interest.

3. Seek self-transcendence.

A disposition of self-transcendence is both an affirmation of the value of life and an action-oriented aspect of hope. It manifests itself in rising above self-interest and difficult circumstances to serve others. These actions of service may be directed upward in terms of serving God and doing his will; or they can flow horizontally in serving one's fellow human beings. Self-transcendence is demonstrated whenever we embrace suffering for the benefit of others. Self-transcendence is shifting the focus from self to serving others. In doing so, one may feel as if he is serving a higher purpose than simply self-interest.

When someone steps outside himself and lets his ego go, he may likely discover an expanded sense of identity, with deeper meaning and wholeness, by connecting more deeply with others.

It is not enough to be your best self. You must give of yourself to others or your life will not be complete.

Serving others can liberate an individual from a miserable existence. Frankl found it very rewarding to encourage his fellow prisoners to find meaning and hope in the midst of their suffering. His "ministry" to the prisoners both stemmed from and reinforced his deeply held belief that meaning can be found in any situation.

By attempting to restore the inner strength of others, he was strengthened. By imparting meaning to others, he found his own life enriched. The essence of self-transcendence is captured concisely in the sentiment expressed by Frankl about his own life. "The meaning of my life," he often would say, "is to help others find the meaning of theirs."[59] Self-transcendence, then, is a tier above Self-actualization. It is not enough to be your best self. You must give of yourself to others or your life will not be complete. Giving of yourself involves creating value, demonstrating unconditional love and leaving a legacy for others. It's going beyond self for the good of others.

4. **Have faith in God and in others.**

For Frankl, hope was inextricably tied to faith. The ancient texts often refer to faith, hope and love as quintessential elements of the human existence. This faith could be characterized as leaning into others for support and strength. Whether one ultimately leans into a higher power or trusts in friendships on a human plane, we each can draw strength from others.

Strong people know that they are finite. So wise finite people turn to the power, provision and knowledge of the infinite.

Faith in God and prayer have been a source of hope for countless individuals in practically hopeless situations. It has been said that man's adversity is God's opportunity. Faith represents a flickering light at the end of the tunnel. Sometimes, it is the only positive expectation in an otherwise dark and hopeless world.

Many people in extreme situations beyond their control resort to hope based on faith in God.

But faith does not have to spring from desperation. Good people always know innately that they are not good enough. Resourceful people always know there are limits to their own resources. Strong people know that they are finite. So wise finite people turn to the power, provision and knowledge of the infinite.

Frankl himself declared: "It is self-evident that belief in a super-meaning – whether as a metaphysical concept or in the religious end of Providence – is of the foremost psychotherapeutic and psychohygienic importance. As a genuine faith springing from inner strength, such a belief adds immeasurably to human vitality."[60]

Some in psychological circles refer to faith-based hope as "the net that catches one when all else fails." Such hope is vested not in oneself but in a higher power, in something more ultimate. One example is the international 12-step tradition of Alcoholics Anonymous, which emphasizes "a power outside of and greater than oneself, that is, a transcendent and in this sense spiritual power."[61] Perhaps it would serve us well to see faith-based hope not as a last resort, but a first choice.

Courage is the capacity to persist in
the face of adversity and failure.

5. **Courageously face and embrace adversity.**

Courage encompasses a host of action-oriented responses to adversity. These responses include the capacity to confront challenges, difficulties and setbacks. Courage is also the stamina to stand one's ground in spite of peer pressure or external force. It entails a commitment to survive in spite of the pain, brutality and hopelessness of any given situation. Courage could be considered the master gland, because without it all other glands will not function well. All else hinges on courage, for it's a reflection of the heroic and defiant human spirit. Acceptance requires courage. Affirmation does too. Stepping out of our personal pain to serve others and serve God also requires the courage to be vulnerable.

We need courage to face the challenges of today. We need courage to face tomorrow with its uncertainty. We need courage to attempt anything, because there is always a risk of opposition and possible failure. Courage is the capacity to persist in the face of adversity and failure. It consists of a combination of commitment, control and challenge. When they occur together, these hardy attitudes facilitate awareness that one can formulate life's meaning for oneself. This meaning is the result of decisions that are made while choosing to be hopeful about the future. The capacity to apply these three elements as aspects of hope can lead to a most vibrant life.[62] In short, courage is manifested in persistence and resourcefulness in striving to attain one's goals, despite anxiety and uncertainty.

Perhaps, in pain we discover the power and meaning of faith.
In our brokenness, we can hear a calling to bring healing
to others.

These five components serve to form the foundation of Frankl's understanding of tragic optimism – or hope. Those who were most likely to survive the Nazi concentration camps were those who had a future meaning to fulfill and had a reason and purpose for living in spite of unbearable suffering. Perhaps, in pain we discover the power and meaning of faith. In our brokenness, we can hear a calling to bring healing to others. In our suffering, it is still possible to encounter joy and serenity. And in our fears and vulnerability, we discover defiant, heroic courage. Sometimes the worst of times can bring out the best in us, if we are committed to personal growth and seek to find deeper meaning in life. Frankl taught us that from the depths of despair we can soar to majestic heights on the wings of hope.

Forget Calm – Be Courageous

In 2000, Stuart Manley, co-owner of Barter Books Ltd. in Alnwich, Northumberland, was sorting through a box of second-hand books bought at auction. Underneath the books, he discovered a copy of one of the original "Keep Calm and Carry On" posters. He framed it and hung it by the cash register. It attracted so much attention that Manley began to produce and sell copies. In late 2005, *Guardian* journalist Susie Steiner featured the replica posters as a Christmas gift suggestion, raising their profile further. Other companies followed Manley's example and the design rapidly began to be used as the theme for a wide range of products. Mary

Manley, Stuart's wife, later commented, "I didn't want it trivialized; but of course, it's been trivialized beyond belief."[63]

Trivialized, indeed, it has been. The poster was meant to be an evocation of British self-discipline, fortitude and a call to remain calm in the midst of chaos. It was intended as an inspirational message at a time of imminent threat of assault. However, it hardly saw the light of day when England was experiencing some of the darkest hours of its history. Because it didn't resonate emotionally with the people, it was never commissioned. Thought by many to be patronizing and divisive, the 2.5 million copies were eventually ground into pulp. It would do us well to remember that in times of adversity, patronizing platitudes are non-productive. People need something of real substance to sustain them. And it should also be noted that peacetime plans won't work under the darkened skies of war.

Tough times require a combination of brutal honesty and credible hope.

Tough times require a combination of brutal honesty and credible hope. Tough times require tough people. And tough people take courageous action. It may be necessary to go to war to ward off the enemies of hopelessness, helplessness, discouragement and depression. If you find yourself waging war to liberate yourself from captors who threaten to kill your very soul, be sure that you go into battle fully armed with hope. Then, forget calm – be courageous!

TEN

What Does This Now Make Possible?

Rise above the storm, and you will find the sunshine.

- MARIO FERNANDEZ

It was a blessing in disguise. But few saw it that way initially. Born into a working-class family in Dublin, in 1932, Christy Brown had twenty-two siblings. Of them, thirteen lived and nine died in infancy. Christy was born with cerebral palsy and unable to move any part of his body other than his left foot. His neurological disorder left him almost entirely spastic in his limbs. Though urged to commit him to a hospital for permanent care, his mother was doggedly determined to raise him at home with their other children.

The dedication and undying love of his mother, Bridget, allowed him to flourish against all odds. She spent countless hours helping him learn to read and write in a time when education for the disabled was simply not an option. During Christy's adolescence, social worker Katriona Delahunt became aware of his plight and began to visit the family regularly. She would bring young Christy books and painting materials, as he demonstrated a keen interest in both the arts and literature. It soon became apparent that Christy possessed a brilliant mind trapped inside a broken body.

With the passage of time, Brown began to demonstrate extremely impressive physical dexterity, learning to both write and draw with the only limb over which he had control – his left foot. Though he received almost no formal schooling during his youth, he quickly matured into a serious artist. Christy was introduced to Robert Collins, a noted author, who soon recognized that Brown was a natural novelist like himself. He used his connections to help Brown publish *My Left Foot*, his long-gestating autobiographical account of his personal struggles with everyday life amidst the vibrant culture of Dublin.[64]

My Left Foot became an international literary sensation and was translated into fourteen languages. Brown became a renowned celebrity and went on to write a series of poetry collections and other novels, including his magnum opus, *Down All the Days*. *The Irish Times* reviewer Bernard Share hailed *Down All the Days* as "the most important Irish novel since *Ulysses*." A film adaptation of *My Left Foot* was produced in 1989, garnering two Academy Awards and a total of five nominations.

Your setback may be the setup for your comeback. There are immense possibilities that lie on the other side of your problems.

In the fashion of Helen Keller, Brown overcame what he couldn't do by focusing on what he could do. He didn't see himself as disabled. Rather he approached life as *differently-abled*. Though he was dogged by the demons of excessive drinking and depression, he became an inspiration to millions worldwide. Through the loving support and encouragement of his mother and a dedicated therapist, he came to have a far-reaching impact and extraordinary notoriety.

What may be bitter trials are often blessings in disguise. Sometimes, you never learn what talents you've got until you're forced to adapt and overcome what may appear to be a handicap. Your next big problem might very well be what sets you on a trajectory that will take you to unimaginable heights. Your setback may be the setup for your comeback. There are immense possibilities that lie on the other side of your problems.

The Pivotal Question

It's a powerful question that causes everything to bend. This single question holds the capacity to change a person's trajectory. While embracing reality, it shifts the focus away from past and present problems and allows the imagination to play with the possibilities. It challenges anyone to choose a productive future, making good personal choices and taking responsibility for them. The question that changes everything is, "What does this now make possible?"

> *The question that changes everything is,*
> *"What does this now make possible?"*

Until an adversity or hardship is encountered, we each are on a chosen path. When circumstances shift and it becomes apparent that our path of choice simply will not work – or no longer exists – then an alternate route must be taken. This ability to adjust and demonstrate agility as you move along life's highway is what we call *pathway thinking*. It's the ability to alter course when necessary. It's the capacity to unsaddle yourself from a dying horse and find a fresh steed. It's grieving what was lost and moving on with your eyes on the horizon. It's dreaming a new dream and exploring new possibilities. It's choosing to fully embrace hope.

As we have seen, hope involves the head, the heart and hands. It's important that all three be fully engaged in order to maximize hopefulness. While there is no surefire seven-step formula to increase hope, a few suggestions may be helpful. In order to most effectively lean into these three arenas, I would offer the following ten guiding ideas for your consideration and application. By putting the following principles into practice, you will be able to experience your hope rising.

1. **Hope requires a plan, so set inspirational goals.**

   Hope begins by setting a course of action. Hope without a plan is nothing more than wishful thinking. Much has been written about the process of goal-setting. I will not be redundant here. If you need a more granular approach to goal-setting, then resources abound. Rather than discussing the details, I prefer to address the larger issue of how goals must tie into personal passion.

   Whether you are an individual wanting to advance in an area that holds great personal value or you are a corporate leader wanting to rally the workforce, the more inspiring your goal, the more enthusiasm it will evoke. A goal has to resonate with the soul in order to move the body. Simply stated it must significantly tie into your values. The more personal, the more impactful. On a individual level, the goal must be an expression of that which is important to you. Set a goal that captivates your attention and stimulates your soul. On a corporate level, it becomes a bit trickier.

In order for a project to be executed effectively,
it must tie corporate objectives to personal values.

In order for a project to be executed effectively, it must tie corporate objectives to personal values. A corporate goal such as "to become the leader in our industry" may sound grandiose, but it lacks individual appeal. It smacks of being impractical and impersonal. Every organization worth its salt should aspire to be a leader in their field. If they don't, then they aren't going to attract or retain top talent. Good players want to be on a championship team. However, this kind of broad, general aspiration does little to evoke personal passion.

A goal, to be inspirational, must tap into what's important to the individuals who comprise the enterprise. Corporate and personal values must be aligned. Here is where the culture of the organization comes into play. Each organization has a culture, or a commitment as to how they intend to interact that is grounded by a common purpose. Culture could be described as how people play together in the sandbox of life. What rules do they follow? What is their common purpose? How will they share their toys? How will they create value? Will they collaborate? Why are they here and what are they here to do? These are all questions of culture. That culture will either be focused on value creation or value extraction.

A culture based on value extraction will possess a what's-in-it-for-me mentality. Each person will be motivated by personal gain. Corporate structures will be driven primarily by competition. A command-and-control leadership style will abound. Here titles and chain of command are greatly valued. In these environments, only the strong survive. It's every man for himself. Such a culture is driven by a scarcity mentality that forces everyone to rush to the table to get as much as they can for themselves. This kind of culture may produce stellar individual performance, but lacks the ability to coalesce teams.

On the contrary, an organization grounded by value creation is based upon an abundance mentality. Here, there is a belief that if we all work together and each person brings more to the table than they take away, at the end of the day there will be a surplus left on the table. This surplus can then be shared by all who were responsible for creating the additional value. This value creation mindset is others-focused. It's based on providing a product or a service that truly makes a difference in people's lives. A value creation culture is about doing good. That good positively impacts clients both internally and externally. It serves to create a greater good and seeks to improve the lives of everyone involved. It's a culture that is passionately driven by a purpose that goes beyond self.

No one is highly motivated to simply make more money for the organization. People innately want to do good. And doing good for others is central to any successful business. An inspirational goal must go beyond simply an attempt to "be the best." It must find its foundation in doing good and making a positive difference in the lives of those that it touches. A value creation orientation will create capacity to rally broad participation and garner high levels of engagement and morale. Make sure that your goals are focused on doing good for everyone that you encounter. People like to do good business with businesses that do good. Organizations that focus on value creation, attract and retain top talent. And they become leaders within their field.

2. **Surround yourself with optimistic, hopeful people.**

As we have seen, going it alone can be deadly. We all need to be connected with others within the context of a loving and supportive community. This is the *With* circle that envelopes everything related to hope. Whom we choose to allow to join us on our journey will determine, to a great extent, whether or not we arrive at our desired destination.

The people around you will either drain or invigorate you. Those who provide encouragement and wise counsel are invaluable to your health and well-being. Those who are negative, critical and constantly exasperating must be kept at bay. This is where boundaries come into play.

Boundaries designate property lines. It's your responsibility to maintain your own emotional backyard. Like a fence separates your yard from others and establishes boundaries, you must erect emotional boundaries to keep trespassers out. Don't let negative people and naysayers dump their emotional garbage in your backyard. That's why there is a gate in the fence. A gate allows good things to come in and keeps bad things out. Close the gate on those who would rob you of hope. Open it to those who prove themselves to be good neighbors. Be careful to neither become isolated nor codependent. Cultivate healthy relationships by connecting appropriately with those who are life-givers. Surround yourself with balcony people who will lift you up when you are feeling down.

Make sure that you surround yourself with people who believe the best in you, want the best for you and expect the best from you.

Make sure that you surround yourself with people who believe the best in you, want the best for you and expect the best from you. You need cheerleaders in your life who will wave the pom-poms for you when you need encouragement most. Recovery groups are essentially founded upon this kind of support system. Fellowships are comprised of groups of individuals, providing a network of encouragement. In addition to the group itself, participants usually have a personal sponsor whose responsibility is to walk with them closely throughout the process. Healthy relationships are essential for recovery from substance abuse. They are also critical in the recovery of hope.

Find or create your own network of supportive relationships. Ask someone to be your sponsor or mentor, guiding you and helping you grow. We each need people in our lives who have access to our garage. People who know where all our junk is stored and can help us move it to create room for what is most valuable. Choose carefully to whom you give the code to your garage. It may determine whether that which is valuable will be protected from stormy weather or left out in the elements.

3. **Get a jumpstart by establishing routines.**

    Anxiety can be paralyzing. Loneliness, depression and traumatic stress can render a person depleted of the energy to move forward. In trying and tumultuous times, it is important to establish a rhythm of activity. Routines, created by lacing together a series of small steps, can serve to automatically start your engine. If you find it difficult to get up and moving in the morning, set the alarm for a specific time and get out of bed as soon as it goes off and brew some coffee. Do it like clockwork. It may be all you need to jumpstart the day. Find a morning ritual that gets you moving.

    The more you create routines,
    the less choices you have to make.

    The more you create routines, the fewer choices you have to make. If you establish a routine of going to the gym three days a week at a certain time, then go. Don't allow yourself to question whether or not you want to go. Don't debate yourself. It's your routine. Go. By eliminating choices, you put yourself on a kind of autopilot which keeps you moving and momentum building.

    As is often said, showing up is half the battle. Sometimes the best thing you can do is just start. Don't worry about anything other than the task right in front of you. It may be a simple task or small step – just do it. Procrastination is often the response to feeling overwhelmed or hopeless. If that's how you feel, then just take baby steps. Baby steps will eventually lead to giant leaps, once you get your footing. Don't just sit there. Establish routines and rituals. Get going and soon you will create a rhythm of activity that will engage your mind, emotions and will.

4. **Create a Life Purpose Statement to guide you.**

The North Star, also known as Polaris, is the most important star in the sky. Because of its importance, one might think that it's also the brightest. But it's not. In fact, it pales in comparison to many other stars, coming in at forty-eighth in terms of brightness. Polaris is so important because Earth's axis points almost directly at it. This means that during the course of the night, Polaris remains in virtually the same spot above the northern horizon year-round, while the other stars circle around it. It neither rises nor sets, providing a constant point of reference by which to navigate. It can always be found in a due northerly direction.

The North Star has been the saving grace for many sailors who may have temporarily lost their way at sea. Its constant position provides clear direction when attempting to plot a course. It allows a vessel sailing at night to maintain its bearing no matter how strong the current or how high the waves. It's a constant beacon in the northern sky.

Passion serves as an individual's personal Polaris,
giving direction to their decision-making.
Passion is the pivotal point around which
all other considerations revolve.

Passion serves as an individual's personal Polaris, giving direction to their decision-making. Passion is the pivotal point around which all other considerations revolve. Passion shows someone's values and establishes their priorities. And one's priorities are the surefire path to productivity. A life purpose statement can codify a person's values and passion in a simple declaration. A life purpose statement is a concise, clear and compelling expression of what's important and what value someone desires to bring to life. This kind of manifesto can provide inspiration and keep someone pointed in the right direction. It can serve as a reminder to stay focused on the right things. When someone's course is altered by circumstances, it can help them self-correct and regain their bearings.

If you've never attempted to do so, take some time to craft a life purpose statement. It should be a vibrant expression of your values. It can incorporate your passion and state clearly what you aspire to do to create value. It can be a statement to which you refer, should you temporarily lose your way. It can serve to bring you back to center. A life purpose statement can become your mantra that keeps you motivated to pursue your purpose with passion. If you haven't already done so, look for the link at the end of Part One, where you can receive guidance on how to write a meaningful life purpose statement. Once you've written it, post it for quick reference until you commit it to memory. Let it become your Polaris.

If we can grow more comfortable with being uncomfortable,
then vulnerability has the potential to transform itself into joy.

5. Vulnerability is courageous, so ask for help.

In her book *Daring Greatly*, Brene Brown describes vulnerability as "uncertainty, risk and emotional exposure." It's that unsettled feeling we get when we step out of our comfort zone or do something that forces us to lose our sense of control. According to Brown, "vulnerability is the core, the heart, the center of meaningful experiences." Drawing from her insights gleaned from twelve years of research in studying vulnerability and shame, Brown shares that what scares us is sometimes actually good for us. If we can grow more comfortable with being uncomfortable, then vulnerability has the potential to transform itself into joy.[65]

Debunking the myth that vulnerability is a sign of weakness, Brown builds the case that it often evokes great courage. Facing and embracing vulnerability – in spite of fear and uncertainty – and choosing to move out of one's comfort zone is actually a bold move. It's also the birthplace of love, belonging, joy, empathy and creativity. Insecurity is present in all of us and is often so strong that we go out of our way to avoid it. However, allowing ourselves to be vulnerable connects us with the rest of humanity and can be the first step toward transformational growth.

Rather than fleeing painful or stressful situations, take an assessment of what you are feeling. Be mindful of the space between where you are emotionally and where you want to be. Then, ask for help to get there. Don't worry about what other people may think. And drop the pretense of being perfect. No one is. So, acknowledge when you are struggling and ask a trusted confidant to be your "pickup rider."

A pickup rider is the person on horseback who works at a rodeo in rough stock competitions. When a bull rider, or someone riding saddle bronc or bareback needs assistance to dismount, the pickup rider comes alongside. Working skillfully, they assist the rider in their dismount by allowing him to exit the bucking fury and find safety. If the rider becomes tangled or caught up in the equipment, a pickup rider is there to assist in freeing the competitor. When faced with bucking fury, we all need a friend, mentor, coach or confidant we can trust to help us dismount safely. And sometimes we need someone to get us untangled from constricting circumstances, before being drug through the dirt. We all could use a pickup rider. So, ask for help.

Being honest with yourself is authenticity.
Being honest with others is transparency.
Vulnerability requires both.

Asking for help requires being honest both with yourself and with others. Being honest with yourself is authenticity. Being honest with others is transparency. Vulnerability requires both. In spite of fear, uncertainty and the emotional exposure that comes from being vulnerable, step out of your comfort zone and be courageous. You may find great encouragement and support in being open with others. And, in doing so, you will most likely find others who have experienced something similar. In fact, it is a truism that the more personal you believe something to be, the more universal it actually is. Vulnerability connects each of us with the rest of humanity.

6. **Celebrate small victories and express gratitude.**

When you experience a victory, then celebrate it no matter how small it may be. Most progress comes incrementally. When we acknowledge that we are making progress, then we can begin to build emotional momentum. As victories are identified and appreciated, then you can begin to build a loop of positive feedback. Celebration of any advancement elevates the energy level and can fuel the next step. Fueled with hope, the next step is more likely to be successful. Seeing progress and celebrating it can be a powerful motivator, as it builds confidence in future possibilities.

One way to celebrate is to acknowledge the contributions that others have made on your behalf. Expressing appreciation makes you mindful of the love and sacrifices that others have made to invest in your development. Stopping to celebrate your relationships and express appreciation to others is powerful. Not only does it acknowledge their gift of time and energy given to you, but it also shows them the impact their love for you has made. Without expression from you, they may never realize how impactful their actions have been. And celebrating others takes the focus off of you and allows you to see the benefit of being others-focused.

Being others-focused will change the way you live. Believe it or not, life isn't about you. You aren't the center of the universe. Life is about us – all of us. We are all in this together. And we are all interconnected. Oh, I know everyone wants to be the lead actor in their own autobiography. But the reality is that you are the result of a number of other factors and significant contributions. That's not to say that you aren't responsible for who you are and where you are. It is simply acknowledging the reality that many people and life experiences have brought you to where you are today. That does not make you a victim of circumstance. However, we each are shaped by the good and bad experiences of life, including how we choose to define suffering.

We provide suffering with definition and meaning
by how we interpret it. How we respond to it gives it power.

Suffering actually serves a purpose. Suffering itself is neutral. It is simply a part of the human experience. We provide suffering with definition and meaning by how we interpret it. How we respond to it gives it power. That power can either crush us under the weight of an unbearable burden, or it can build stamina and strength of character if we refuse to succumb to the pressure. So, even the bad things that happen can be transformed into positive results.

I am personally grateful for life experiences that were tough because they compelled me to take alternate routes that turned out to be for the good. It may sound strange, but I have actually celebrated defeats because ultimately, they have led to opportunities that were better than anything I could have imagined. Without the trial or setback that pushed me down other paths,

I would have never voluntarily chosen those paths for myself. So, not only can you celebrate small victories and other people, but you can also celebrate defeats when you have the hope that tomorrow can be brighter than yesterday or today.

7. **Invest in yourself and in others.**

The concept of investment is grounded in the idea of creating value. You don't willfully invest in a lost cause. You don't invest to lose money. The hope is that your investment of time, energy and money will eventually have a payoff. We understand this from a financial standpoint, but we often fail to see this from a relational standpoint. To build wealth, you have to make investments.

When an investment pays off, we say it has matured. If you purchase a bond, the maturity date is the time that your investment is paid to you in full with interest. But with people, there is no maturity date. Growth is a constant process throughout our lifetime. One can never honestly say that they have reached maturity, for growth is literally a lifelong process.

So, how are you investing in your personal growth and development? And how are you investing in others? The unfortunate reality is that many folks never stop to give consideration to whether or not they are moving toward maturity. Create value by investing intentionally in yourself. This may mean exploring new activities and endeavors that would bring a sense of accomplishment or pleasure. For others, it may mean helping them connect with the resources or relationships that could enhance their endeavors. Most people are only a few introductions away from seeing a dream become a reality. You may be able to assist in making that connection.

Everything worthwhile in life is a byproduct
of creating value for others.

The interesting thing about investing in others is that it pays off personally. The best way to learn something is to teach someone else. The fastest way to success is to make those around you successful. If you want to be happy, do what you can to ensure the happiness of those closest to you. Everything worthwhile in life is a byproduct of creating value for others.

Viktor Frankl affirmed this idea when he wrote, "Don't aim at success – the more you aim at it and make it a target, the more you are going to miss it. For success, like happiness, cannot be pursued; it must ensue, and it only does so as the unintended side-effect of one's dedication to a cause greater than oneself or as the by-product of one's surrender to a person other than oneself. Happiness must happen, and the same holds for success: you have to let it happen by not caring about it. I want you to listen to what your conscience commands you to do and go on to carry it out to the best of your knowledge. Then you will live to see that in the long run – in the long run, I say – success will follow you precisely because you had *forgotten* to think of it."[66]

8. **Assess the situation honestly and re-goal when appropriate.**

Hope never denies reality. It doesn't help to postpone the inevitable by sticking your head in the sand. Refusing to see a situation for what it actually is can delay or diminish hope for a positive outcome. Sometimes it becomes necessary to let go of that which is not working in order to pursue better prospects. Making necessary adjustments in a timely fashion can be the difference between a project flourishing or dying on the vine.

Hope never denies reality. It doesn't help to postpone the inevitable by sticking your head in the sand.

I enjoy hanging out around vineyards. I find the whole process of growing grapes and making wine fascinating – and delectable. There is a simple principle that must be followed in order for any vineyard to be successful. You must prune the vine in order for it to be productive. Left untended, vines can become unwieldy and unable to ripen a large crop or sustain adequate vegetative growth. The purpose of pruning is to obtain maximum yields of high-quality grapes and to allow adequate vegetative growth for the following season.

Assessing a situation accurately and re-goaling demonstrates agility and an ability to prune what is dead. Flexibility to choose a viable alternative is the outcome of good pathway thinking. When it becomes clear that one route is impassable, it becomes futile to attempt to force your way through with brute strength. Nothing of long-lasting positive value is ever accomplished by force. You may be able to garner initial results by bullying your way through, but the repercussions will eventually turn negative. People resist being coerced. Every force in nature is met with an equally resistant force. Isaac Newton's third law of motion could be stated as follows: "For every action, there is an equal and opposite reaction. When one body pushes against another, the second body pushes back just as hard."[67] This is not only true in physics, but it's also true relationally.

Brute force, ultimately, is an act in futility. Sometimes it's better to cut bait and minimize your losses so you can live to fish another day in another pond. Sometimes you have to let go and grieve the loss. Grieving is the soul's way of metabolizing life's experiences. When you ingest food, the body uses what is beneficial and eliminates the rest in waste. Grieving does the same thing. It helps you celebrate the good and eliminate the bad from your consciousness. We have to learn to effectively digest difficulty. Re-goaling helps you retain the good and release that which does not or cannot work.

Sometimes you have to let go and grieve the loss.
Grieving is the soul's way of metabolizing life's experiences.

In setting a different goal or a new direction, hope can be renewed. The destination may have changed, but the personal value has increased because the likelihood of success is greater. It's a funny thing, but people often prefer a problem that they can't solve to a solution that they don't like. Don't carry such baggage. It may not be preferable, but it may become necessary to jettison cargo that may be weighing you down and set your sails for a new heading. Assess each situation honestly and make adjustments accordingly.

9. **Focus on what you can do to increase personal power.**

There is much in life over which we have no control. Life happens. Of course, positive results can be garnered by responsible actions. However, sometimes life just hits the fan. Bad things can occur with or without our help. When we are responsible for creating a bad situation, our behavior should be addressed and changed to avoid negative consequences. But there are times that circumstances beyond our control put us in unpleasant positions. At these times, it's helpful to focus on those things over which we do have influence or control.

You cannot control that which you cannot control.
*So, do what you **can** do.*

To state the obvious, you cannot control that which you cannot control. So, do what you *can* do. You cannot control the economy unless, of course, you are the Chairman of the Federal Reserve. You cannot control other people, so all attempts to threaten, manipulate or shame anyone into doing anything must be abandoned. Such tactics will only lead to a relational wasteland. If you are honest with yourself, there isn't much in life that you can control other than yourself.

A sense of personal power comes through responsible action. Responsible action means working on you. We can't always choose our circumstances, but we can choose how we respond to those circumstances. In other words, we do not always decide on what circumstances may come our way but we can define them. We can choose our attitude and how we respond to them. It's the best expression of human liberty. It is the defiant power of the human spirit.

Again, I turn to Frankl for insight as he writes:

"But what about human liberty? Is there no spiritual freedom in regard to behavior and reaction to any given surroundings? Is that theory true which would have us believe that man is no more than a product of many conditional and environmental factors – be they of biological, psychological or sociological nature? Is man but an accidental product of these? Most important, do the prisoners' reactions to the singular world of the concentration camp prove that man cannot escape the influences of his surroundings? Does man have no choice of action in the face of such circumstances?

We can answer these questions from experience as well as on principle. The experiences of camp life show that man does have a choice of action. There were enough examples, often of a heroic nature, which proved that apathy could be overcome, irritability suppressed. Man can preserve a vestige of spiritual freedom, of independence of mind, even in such terrible conditions of psychic and physical stress.

We who lived in concentration camps can remember the men who walked through the huts comforting others, giving away their last piece of bread. They may have been few in number, but they offer sufficient proof that everything can be taken from a man but one thing: the last of the human freedoms – to choose one's attitude in any given set of circumstances, to choose one's own way.

And there were always choices to make. Every day, every hour, offered the opportunity to make a decision, a decision which determined whether you would or would not submit to those powers which threatened to rob you of your very self, your inner freedom; which determined whether or not you would become the plaything of circumstance, renouncing freedom and dignity to become molded into the form of the typical inmate."[68]

Focusing on what you can do and taking responsible action is the greatest exercise in expressing your human liberty.

Focusing on what you can do and taking responsible action is the greatest exercise in expressing your human liberty. Don't be conformed to the surroundings of your circumstances. Rather, be transformed by the renewing of your mind by exercising your freedom to rise above the circumstances. We are all capable of changing the world for the better when possible, and responsible for changing ourselves for the better when necessary. Whether or not we reach our potential in life is determined by our choices, not our conditions or chance.

We are all capable of changing the world for the better when possible, and responsible for changing ourselves for the better when necessary. Whether or not we reach our potential in life is determined by our choices, not our conditions or chance.

10. **You gotta have faith.**

It's interesting that in many ancient religious texts you will often see faith, hope and love cited together. In many ways, they are inextricably linked. They form a dynamic spiritual triad. But what is most fascinating is that none of these may be commanded or ordered on demand. Rather, they are each realized in a most indirect way.

Love is the only way to grasp another human being at the core of who they are. No one can fully know another unless he loves him.

Love is the only way to grasp another human being at the core of who they are. No one can fully know another unless he loves him. This love enables someone to see essential traits in another that remain unseen by others who only know that person casually.

At the same time, love allows someone to see potential in someone else that has yet to be actualized. By this love, the loving person enables the loved one to actualize those potentialities. By believing in him and making him aware of what he can be and should become, he makes these possibilities come true.

To a great extent, we each define and bring meaning to our own existence by our choices and actions.

Likewise, faith opens us up to possibilities beyond self. When a person relies wholly on oneself, he soon discovers that by himself he has a limited capacity in what he can make of himself. As we have said, it is true that one must demonstrate extreme responsibility in growing to fulfill one's potential. To a great extent, we each define and bring meaning to our own existence by our choices and actions. But there is also an awareness in the depths of the human soul that we have a limited capacity to fulfill our potential and chart our destiny. There is a void in the human spirit that craves a connection – with others and with God. Whether believer or not, there is an unsettling suspicion that there must be more to life than our limited human experience. Faith allows the possibility to connect with the divine and to experience the unseen. Faith, then, opens the door to the reality that there are resources available beyond oneself.

And, as for hope, it springs from a spirit infused with love and faith. While we can understand some of the mechanics involved in generating it, and we can apply principles that can accelerate it, hope dwells in the domain of the divine. In essence, when all is said and done, hope springs eternal from the soul that is not limited by the conflict nor the circumstances of that which is mortal. In order to have the richest of hope, you gotta have faith.

Contained within these ten practices, you will find a balance of applications to more fully engage the head, the heart and the hands. I have set forth three principles from the intrinsic, extrinsic and systemic components respectively. Applying these principles will accelerate the rise of your hope. The tenth, which is faith-oriented, serves both as foundation and capstone.

Ten Practices to Help You Apply Hope

1. Hope requires a plan, so set inspirational goals.
2. Surround yourself with optimistic, hopeful people.
3. Get a jumpstart by establishing routines.
4. Create a Life Purpose Statement to guide you.
5. Vulnerability is courageous, so ask for help.
6. Celebrate small victories and express gratitude.
7. Invest in yourself and in others.
8. Assess the situation honestly and re-goal when appropriate.
9. Focus on what you can do to increase personal power.
10. You gotta have faith.

The Rest of the Story

Christy Brown rose to international fame by applying a handful of these principles. Early in his life he was surrounded by loving and supportive people. He focused on what he could do. He was forced to establish a routine and he celebrated his successes, no matter how small they may have been for others. These few principles turned his tragic life-circumstances into a triumph.

Unfortunately, it didn't last. His disappointments in life and disillusionment with love left him bitter, self-absorbed and self-destructive. Addicted and searching desperately for acceptance, he left the very principles that allowed him to soar to unimaginable heights. He strayed from the very life-giving and life-breathing lessons that gave his life meaning. Knitting together the memories of his siblings and closest friends, a portrait can be painted of a man who lived his later life in an angry, alcoholic haze, married to a prostitute who had affairs and neglected him.

Mary Carr took Christy Brown away from his friends and family and from his beloved Dublin. He ended a 10-year love affair with Beth Moore to be with Carr. Christy left the woman who provided the stability and discipline to draw the best out of him, trading it for someone who gave him momentary pleasure. In his final years, those he was once closest to barely saw him. In the end, Christy died at the age of 49 after choking on a dinner of lamb chops. The bruises found on his body suggest that Carr was abusive in the end.[69]

Abandoning those principles that once brought him hope, Brown allowed his soul to slowly erode away, destroying his art and then himself. Christy Brown was an astonishing man with a brilliant mind trapped in a broken body. He accomplished more than most able-bodied people could ever dream. But he died in isolation and obscurity because he abandoned the principles that once made him great.

ELEVEN

Hope for the Best

There are always flowers for those who want to see them.

- HENRI MATISSE

My brother-in-law is very creative and handy with tools, willing to tackle a myriad of repair and improvement projects around his house. But he is certainly no horticulturist. To say he has a green thumb would be a blatant admission of color-blindness. Though working in the yard is somewhat therapeutic for him, he never bothered to school himself on the flora and fauna of the south. When he and his family moved into their home in Daphne, Alabama, his gardening tools consisted of nothing more than a lawn mower and a weed whacker. His mission was singular – cut it down. He had no interest in cultivating anything in his yard.

Along his fence and across the back of his house was a weedy, tangled mess of thorny undergrowth, ugly to eye and bristly. It was beyond him why someone would allow such an unseemly growth to overtake the borders of the lawn. So he set out to whack it away. But the growth was persistent. Every spring it would come back with a vengeance, seemingly spreading with each subsequent season, until its cane-like shoots consumed the fence line. Frustrated and bewildered, he went to extremes in dealing with the annoying bushy presence. For a lengthy time, he treated it with Roundup, and continued to whack it to the ground. But he found himself fighting a losing battle. He finally gave up in exasperation and just let it grow.

One day while relaxing in the backyard, the spindly vine caught his attention. To his dismay, he noticed what looked like small berries clustered all over the weedy pestilence. What he considered to be such a nuisance turned out to be blackberry vines. What he worked so hard to fight back and cut out of his lawn has now become a delight. Its fruit now fills pies and jelly jars, bringing sweetness and smiles to their lives.

Sometimes the annoyances we want to remove from our lives are the very gifts we have been given to help us grow and make our lives bear sweet fruit.

Sometimes the annoyances we want to remove from our lives are the very gifts we have been given to help us grow and make our lives bear sweet fruit. Our first inclination may be to eradicate nuisances because they are messy and bristly. They are unsightly. They don't fit into our well-manicured lawns or lives. They are a hassle and show no apparent signs of producing anything good. So, we set out to whack them out of our lives. Rather than embrace them, we stiff-arm the struggles to keep them at bay. We try to keep life looking pretty by denying their presence. And, when all else fails, we try to control people and circumstances by brute force to keep life in line. But that never works. Because nothing of long-lasting positive value ever happens by force. People become resistant and resentful when you try to control them. And circumstances don't bend to our desires. They just get messier.

I'm not suggesting that you should allow weeds to grow wildly. If you want a healthy lawn, then you have to remove them. You have to treat and care for your grass if you want to grow a green lawn. The same holds true for our lives and relationships. If you want to grow a strong character, then you have to remove those infestations that would threaten to encroach and choke out good growth. We must do the hard work of introspection and pull up that which is unseemly and seed with good grass. If we don't, then character deficiencies can spread negative consequences as quickly as uncontrolled dandelions can spread throughout a yard.

If you want to grow a strong character, then you have to remove those infestations that would threaten to encroach and choke out good growth.

However, sometimes the things you want to remove may be the very things to help you improve. Challenges are the instruments of fate to round off the rough edges of our character. This is true in marriage, and it is equally true when you are trying to transform society. And ultimately, challenges force you to evaluate issues of life and death.

Hope for a Hopeless Marriage

Rob and Lisa met in Minneapolis. She was a beautiful, successful businesswoman and he had a strong entrepreneurial bent. Both were in their mid-careers. While Lisa had become a partner in her organization, Rob had founded and grown a highly respected enterprise of his own and was a managing partner. Lisa had earned a reputation as a leader in her field, rising to serve as president of the state association for her industry. And Rob enjoyed his responsibilities, growing a flourishing firm which had a far-reaching impact throughout the community and beyond.

When they met, they were both single with children. Lisa had a daughter and Rob, a widower, had three children of his own. They both led busy lives, but longed for the day that they might find someone to share life with again. After a fairy tale courtship, they chose to become a blended family. Soon after they wed, he adopted her daughter and she took on maternal responsibilities for three additional almost-adolescent children. They set out to create a storybook life for themselves, becoming a modern-day version of the Brady Bunch.

Life was blissful for a while. But it didn't take long for reality to set in. The difficulties of dealing with a blended family quickly led to disillusionment for them both. Lisa was a firm disciplinarian, who had strong opinions about how matters should be handled in the home. Rob, on the other hand, was a peacemaker who often enabled bad behavior by making excuses for himself and the children when they acted out. To be fair, the strength that Lisa demonstrated to rise to such a prominent position in an industry dominated by men, was the same strength that put a strain on their marriage. And Rob's ability to navigate and mediate extremely sensitive business negotiations, by illuminating issues on both sides, didn't necessarily work well at home. Soon, the stress in their relationship began to put a strain on their marriage.

To their credit, they were both determined to stick it out and make their marriage work. Neither one of them wanted another broken relationship that would bring further damage. For years, they gutted it out, often finding themselves at odds with one another over various issues. Time took its toll. Rob became disillusioned and Lisa became hopeless that they would ever experience the friendship and intimacy that they had imagined when they first met.

The problem was that they were both trying to change one another. They both had their own issues. Everyone does. Part of the problem was that they both had a tendency to project their personal issues onto the other. Lisa could clearly see Rob's faults and did everything within her power to change him. But she had a hard time seeing herself honestly. At the same time, the very issues that drove Rob crazy about Lisa were the very issues that he struggled with too. But he was so focused on her that he couldn't see them in himself. Rather than each person looking at themselves, they kept trying to fix one another. Their frustration soon turned to exasperation – with the situation and with one another. The topic of divorce began to creep into their conversations.

Trying to change someone else is not merely challenging, it's impossible. Seeing someone else's shortcomings is much easier than seeing them in ourselves.

Trying to change someone else is not merely challenging, it's impossible. Seeing someone else's shortcomings is much easier than seeing them in ourselves. Often our energies and efforts are misdirected when we attempt to control another. What we should be doing is focusing on ourselves. And perhaps our focus, in our relationships with those closest to us, is all wrong to begin with. Maybe we don't clearly understand the greater benefit of fully knowing another and being fully known by another.

What if there is a richer result of an intimate relationship than merely making us happy? What if instead, emotional intimacy is a vehicle through which we can be made whole and healthy? From the time that we are children, we read about storybook relationships where everyone lives happily ever after. But happiness should not be the focus of our relationships. Happiness pursued, eludes. Happiness can only ensue. In other words, if you make happiness your goal, you will never attain it. Happiness is a byproduct of doing what is right and acting responsibly by living according to your values and seeking to create value for others.

> *If you make happiness your goal, you will never attain it.*
> *Happiness is a byproduct of doing what is right and acting*
> *responsibly by living according to your values and*
> *seeking to create value for others.*

When you know another deeply and are fully known by them, then there is an acute awareness of each other's weaknesses. We know where the cracks lie in their character and they know where ours are as well. Unconditional love calls us to accept the other as they are, while encouraging their growth and development. But such encouragement cannot come in the form of coercion, blame or shame. You cannot command the growth of another or force them to adopt your perspective. Instead, you can only extend an invitation and make a commitment to be a role model of good behavior. Encouraging growth in another is only effective when you lead by example.

The challenge is that we are all broken. We all have our own emotional baggage that we bear, packed by life experiences and expectations. When we walk closely with someone, our baggage flops around and can easily get entangled in the baggage of the other, becoming additionally burdensome. The solution is not to address the other person's baggage. Rather, deal with your own, repacking it so that it doesn't impede your growth or the progress of another.

The key to growth is honesty and vulnerability. When you are honest with yourself and others, then you can drop the pretense of perfection and focus on addressing your own shortcomings. Pride produces a pretense that forces someone to posture themselves as being more than they actually are. Humility is the acknowledgment of the frailty of your humanity and the willingness to work on your issues. Trusting relationships provide the context of a safe environment in which one can effectively address sensitive issues of personal growth. This trust is, to a great extent, the result of authenticity and transparency. Authenticity could simply be described as the ability to be honest with yourself. And transparency is the willingness to be honest with others about yourself and the situation. When we are honest with ourselves and others, then growth can take place that can lead to health and wholeness.

When I say wholeness, however, I don't want to leave the wrong impression. Becoming whole is never dependent upon someone else's activity. It is a process that we must own and be personally responsible for creating. About this point, there is a myth that must be dispelled. Many believe that when someone finds that special someone, then their *soul mate* will make them complete and somehow fill the gaps created by their deficiencies. Thus, making them whole and happy.

Many a woman has become misty-eyed while watching the movie Jerry Maguire. A love story wrapped up in the world of athletics and sports agents, it offers something for both genders. In one poignant scene, Jerry (played by Tom Cruise) turns to Dorothy (played by Renee Zellweger) and utters the line that has become famous among females everywhere. Having finally come to the realization that he cannot live without her,

Jerry – in a rare moment of candor – expresses how much he has missed Dorothy and finally utters the words, "I love you. You complete me!" It is a magical moment in movies that is singularly responsible for wasting Kleenex worldwide. While the declaration is certainly sentimental, it has a faulty foundation.

There is no person out there somewhere who has the magical power to complete you. No soul mate will ever be able to satiate the deepest longings of your soul and meet your emotional needs. If you believe the myth, you will either live the rest of your life disappointed or spend the remainder of your days searching for a unicorn that doesn't exist. The world is filled with broken people searching for someone else to make them complete. A sense of purpose and fulfillment can only come from within as a person lives out their values and makes a commitment to personal growth and creating value for others.

A good marriage is a work of art crafted over the course of time by two broken people who recognize their frailty, extend grace to one another and love each other unconditionally.

A good marriage is a work of art crafted over the course of time by two broken people who recognize their frailty, extend grace to one another and love each other unconditionally. Such a relationship is marked by an atmosphere of safety, where each person can be themselves without fear of judgment. There is no reason to hide or pretend because acceptance and affirmation are present. A healthy marriage is a place where support and encouragement are provided for each person to grow to their full potential.

Through the help and counsel of an older couple who mentored them, Rob and Lisa learned to quit focusing on one another. Instead, they worked intently on taking care of their own business. They dealt deeply with their own emotional baggage. And they worked hard at being vulnerable. They were honest with themselves and honest with one another. Though being vulnerable meant emotional exposure and uncertainty, they mustered the courage to acknowledge their weaknesses and struggles to one another.

They began to admit quickly when they were in the wrong and apologized rather than deflecting or blaming each other. And they offered forgiveness without feeling the need to shame the other. They lost the urge to pontificate to drive a point home following an apology. Rather than judge or criticize, they intentionally looked for opportunities to affirm one another whenever they could. And they worked hard to believe the best in one another rather than to expect the worst. Rather than seeing the other as the problem in any situation, they began to move together as allies in facing and addressing the issue at hand. For the first time in a long time, they were playing on the same team. They were unified. And it felt really good.

It took some time, but the smoldering embers of their love began to burn a little brighter. They began to dream again – and to make plans for the future. They began to once again believe that their tomorrow together could be a brighter day and they began to act responsibly to make is so. When faced with challenges, they turned to each other and drew strength from one another. And when there were setbacks and disappointments, they learned to flex and adapt. They set new goals together. An exhilarating sense of anticipation began to grow for the future. What had, at one time, been a marriage on the rocks was now on a course to sail off into a beautiful sunset. Once again, they had hope.

One Race

It's only been a matter of weeks since I started writing this book in the hopes of bringing encouragement to many during a challenging chapter in history. And now, just two months later, the world is convulsing – again. Reactions have been swift and intense over the senseless death of George Floyd, taken at the hands of those who had sworn to protect. Emotions are raw and they run deep. For far too long, we have been a society ripped apart by people who have held to the mistaken notion that the color of a person's skin has anything to do with his character. Racism, in any form, is a symptom of a sick society. It is a deadly virus, transmitted through fear and hatred, that attacks the mind and the soul. It crushes the spirit and chokes the breath out of people. Once again, fear, frustration, anxiety and anger abound. Hopelessness is gaining a foothold on the American psyche.

Peaceful protesters march in cities around the globe to ensure justice for all. Others, with ill intent, incite hatred and violence in self-serving idiocy, minimizing the message. But the message must be heard and heeded. Life is valuable. Every life is important. Everyone who respects others deserves respect. Ethnicity may matter when it comes to your origin, but it should have nothing to do with your destiny. Your destiny is determined by character and choice in a free society.

The work of antiracism is to become better human beings
so that we treat every human being better.

This is not a racial divide. It is a human divide. For we are all one race – the human race. There is no them, only us – we are all in this together. The work of antiracism is to become better human beings so that we treat every human being better.

Tomorrow will be brighter than today only if we all strive to be better people and make better choices. Choices that show respect. Choices that reflect hope. Riots and violence will not shift the human heart for the good. Raging and looting clearly demonstrate that such perpetrators have no dignity and show no respect for others and their property. These are the desperate acts of desperate people who lack hope. Hopeless people feel helpless. They don't believe that they can make a difference. That makes hopeless people the most dangerous in the world. They have nothing to live for, so they rail against. Because they are hopeless, they are willing to compromise their values to make a statement – even if it means taking advantage of and harming others. But violence only begets violence.

We must stop this moral slide. We must restore dignity for our fellow man and respect one another. We must view *all* life as precious. We must pursue justice with a passion. We must diligently practice kindness. We must walk humbly together – hand in hand. We must listen. We must learn. We must see the world differently. Change will never come by rioting and railing *against*. Hope takes a stand *for* that which is valuable. Hope can bring healing to our broken land.

*Life gets messy. Truth is found in the messy middle,
where the screeches of extremism are silenced
and hope can be birthed.*

Hope acknowledges the problem. Life gets messy. Truth is found in the messy middle, where the screeches of extremism are silenced and hope can be birthed. Hope envisions a better tomorrow and crafts a plan to get there. Hope takes aggressive action without being the aggressor. Hope denounces evil, while refusing to fall victim to its destructive clutches. Hope stands toe to toe with injustice and calls it out. Hope listens. Hope seeks to understand. Hope takes action to right wrongs. Hope seeks forgiveness. Hope offers grace. Hope crosses the divide and embraces a brother. Hope brings healing by standing on common ground. Hope finds a solution. Hope discovers a way. Hope unifies humanity. Because hope knows that we are all One Race.

> *"If you lose hope, somehow you lose the vitality that keeps life moving, you lose that courage to be, that quality that helps you go on in spite of it all. And so today I still have a dream."*
>
> **- MARTIN LUTHER KING JR.**

Regi's Story

No matter what path you choose to take in life, you are certain to encounter bumps, turns and detours along the way. When one way becomes no longer viable, then an alternate route must be chosen. And if the road you wanted to take becomes blocked by an insurmountable barrier, then sometimes you have to change the destination as well. Re-goaling is the detour part of the journey. It's the ability to demonstrate agility when what one longs for becomes impossible. It's where hope meets courage.

It was a rare day in Atlanta. Snow covered the parking lot where cars converged for the celebration. Though the weather was inclement, at least by Atlanta standards, thousands of people poured into the auditorium to honor a life well lived. A friend to all and a mentor to most who congregated that day, Regi impacted countless lives for the good. His legacy loomed large. He was as large as life itself. And we were there for one reason. To be uplifted and encouraged by Regi. Though not present, still he was.

But it wasn't your typical funeral service. Oh, sure, it was marked by friends and family sharing their thoughts and memories. There was music, the reading of scripture and a message brought by the pastor who had walked closely with him for years. But what I remember most was the multi-media presentation that had been crafted by Regi himself. Filled with pictures of family and friends, it told the story of a life well lived. A life of few regrets. A life of impact. It contained words of encouragement and admonition, accompanied by a multitude of smiles and zany pictures. It was pure Regi – marked by a dry wit and a Cheshire Cat grin. The reception that followed was held amidst tables overflowing with his favorite food – Krispy Kreme Doughnuts. It was classic Regi. Just like his life, the whole occasion was somber in its challenge, yet light-hearted in its presentation. Laughter, not tears, punctuated the occasion. It was exactly as he had envisioned it.

His death was not altogether unexpected. He had been battling fear-lessly on multiple physical fronts. Diagnosed with pulmonary issues in his forties, Regi silently monitored his situation as it steadily declined. Never one to complain, still he queried doctors occasionally about his experience with shortness of breath. Because of his appearance, doctors were optimistic in their prognosis. However, his test results belied his beaming countenance. Time took its toll and eventually Regi had to undergo a lung transplant operation. Affectionately named *Larry*, his new lung gave him a new lease on life. Initially, Regi was a poster child for transplant success. But lung transplants are tenuous. Because the lungs are an organ constantly exposed to the environment and susceptible to many conditions, the body has an acute inclination toward rejection. Caring for *Larry* would have been challenging for anybody. But the fire would soon intensify.

Three years after the lung transplant, Regi was diagnosed with Merkel Cell Carcinoma, a rare and often rapidly-spreading form of skin cancer. Though initial treatments seemed successful, it subsequently reappeared in the lymph nodes of his neck. The Merkel Cell Carcinoma had metastasized behind Regi's ear. On top of that, *Larry* the lung had started to fail. A neck dissection was performed to remove the lymph nodes, but soon the cancer returned with a vengeance, leaving Regi in a tight spot. If they treated the cancer, it would compromise his immune system and almost certainly cause his body to reject the lung. If they treated the lung, it would feed the cancer. It was a conundrum with life and death ramifications.

Being faced with what seemed to be inevitable, Regi pivoted. In facing the insurmountable, he altered course. He re-goaled. Living a longer life seemed to have been taken off the table. Rather than wish the situation to be different, he faced reality and became more intentional. He drew concentric circles of his relationships and began to invest his remaining time wisely.

The outer circle consisted of the men he had invested in so freely. By everyone's accounting, over the last twenty years of his life, Regi had personally mentored over 160 men in small groups of eight. Those, in turn, had gone on to impact thousands of other lives. Regi had made an immense positive wake in the world and changed countless lives as he provided marital, professional and spiritual counsel. In his final days, he wanted to give many of them a parting challenge. He dedicated some of his time to them. He challenged each one of them to live life to the fullest. And he did so, leading by example. In fact, he led his final mentoring meeting on the Monday night before his death on Friday.

The next circle was his extended family. For them, he provided letters, spoken words of encouragement and recordings to mark special memories. He was creating for them a legacy that would live on long after he parted. And then, the tightest circle was for his wife, Miriam, and his children. He relished celebrating their fiftieth wedding anniversary, as they reminisced about how wonderful their lives together had been. Their marriage, while it hadn't been perfect, was filled with grace and growth for both of them. He wrote lengthy letters for each of his children and grandchildren. In each hand-written letter, he pronounced a mixture of blessings and encouragement, recounting the lessons that he wanted them to remember. And, having had to pivot in his plans, Regi made for himself a reminder of his personal commitments, lest he forget how he should focus. His commitment board represented his attempt at re-goaling. This is what was scrawled across a large flip chart that he kept close-by:

COMMITMENTS

- I WILL WALK WITH JESUS EVERY DAY.
- I WILL BE GRATEFUL AND LIVE EVERY DAY TO THE FULLEST.
- I WILL BLESS MY FAMILY WITH WORDS, PICTURES AND VIDEOS.
- I WILL INVEST IN "MY GUYS" FOR THEIR GOOD – GOD'S GLORY – NOT MINE.
- I WILL NOT GIVE UP AND "RUN OUT THE CLOCK."
- I WILL LET PEOPLE LOVE ON ME!

When I first saw Regi's board, a few thoughts jumped off his page and into my heart. I'm sure that's just as Regi intended. Not only did he want these words to guide his daily decisions, but he also wanted them to inspire others. First, I noticed it was written in all capital letters. Regi never lacked for boldness and his words were important – to him, and for all of us. Secondly, the word *WILL* represents a choice. Regi was no victim of life's circumstances. He refused to be defined by his physical struggles. And he certainly wasn't defined by his failures. In fact, he would often admit that his failures eventually led to greatness, once he got out of his own way. He chose to define life on his terms. He had a *Will* crafted by hope. And, because of hope, he lived as a grateful man.

The most obvious was that when the prognosis turned bleak, and long-term goals had to be abandoned, he chose to re-goal on a day-to-day basis. He was going to live each and every day to the fullest. And his hope required him to get a plan. His plan was to lean into his faith, his friends and his family. He wanted to grow spiritually by connecting more intimately with his God. He wanted to love his family more fully. He wanted to leave them with wonderful memories and bless them with the legacy of a life that could be celebrated. And he desired to invest more deeply in the men that he was mentoring, creating as much value for them as he possibly could in the time he had remaining.

Regi understood the importance of *With*. He relished in the joy of community. He surrounded himself with optimistic, hope-filled people who either had faith or were pursuing faith. Investing in relationships was his highest priority. In the end, he let those to whom he had given so much of himself, give back to him in return.

As the inevitable approached, those who loved him most deeply witnessed one of the kindest death experiences possible. In the final days, he was surrounded by friends and family, celebrating special times. He was lucid until the last day. Never complaining, the only time he wept was with joy over how good life and God had been to him. He cried only out of gratitude. And among his final words, he often repeated, "I cannot believe I get to see Jesus. He changed my life. He changed everything." His hope went far beyond this earth.

Regi was larger than life itself. He loved every minute of it. He died as he lived, full of faith, hope and love. As a result, he left an indelible mark on his world. His legacy will long be remembered as remarkable by those who knew him. Regi's life, death and afterlife were all marked by hope. When the end was inevitable, he was at peace. He knew it was his time to go. He knew he was going to a better place. For Regi, his life on earth had come to an end. Even then, he believed that his tomorrow would be brighter. He had no fear of death. He knew heaven awaited him on the other side. He had hope.

Even on his dying day, Regi held the confident belief that his tomorrow would be better. No matter how bleak today may seem, maybe we, too, can possess the hope on a non-dying day that our tomorrow can be brighter.

TWELVE

Rising to the Occasion

All endings are also beginnings.
We just don't know it at the time.

- MITCH ALBOM

O n one of our trips to the wine country of California, my wife and
I made plans to take a hot air balloon ride over the lush vineyards
of the surrounding hills and valleys. The morning of our aerial
adventure, the weather was cool and moderately breezy. As the sun rose
over the rolling hills, we arrived at the launch location in time to watch
the crew make preparations for our flight. It was a fascinating sight to see.

Dual propane burners, capable of producing thirty-six million BTUs
of heat per hour, were blasting hot air into an enormous multi-colored
envelope. As the behemoth awoke from its slumber, it began to take shape
and waft gently in the morning breeze. When the big bright bag had
harnessed enough heat, it began to slowly rise. The crew scrambled to
tether it to the ground, lest it float away. Passengers quickly boarded
and the balloon was released from its shackles. Floating free from the

restraints of being earthbound, we took flight into a cloudless sky. It was mesmerizing.

The first thing I noticed during our ascent was that the breezes which were so apparent on the ground were now gone. Because we were being carried by them, we could no longer feel their effect. The only way we knew the breezes were still blowing was by marking the speed of our travel as we passed objects on the ground. In the basket, it was eerily calm and peaceful. It was surreal.

The morning ride, though it lasted for hours, seemed to go by in a matter of minutes. Rising and falling at our pilot's will, we were carried on the now brisk breezes across the hill country, enjoying the breathtaking beauty of the lush landscape below. From our elevated perspective, life looked different. It was calm; it was peaceful. We had risen above the chaos and clamor of the activity on the ground. We were untethered from the restrictions of our earthbound existence. We floated freely on the winds.

Though our course had been charted before launch, our final landing spot was chosen by circumstances beyond our control. Wind currents and landscape determined our final destination. Given those variables, our drop zone changed a number of times before our trip finally came to an end. On the ground, our chase team scrambled to keep up, flexing to our ever-changing flight. When the conditions were right and an opening in the terrain identified, we made our final descent. Eventually landing far-removed from our original destination, we had created a memorable experience. One that I have often pondered and from which I have gleaned some powerful principles.

There are a number of lessons to be taken from that hot air balloon experience. That sunny, breezy morning in Napa, I learned that in order to rise, you must first harness the heat. The burners used to inflate the balloon produced enough heat to incinerate everything in the immediate area. Yet the experienced crew was able to capture what otherwise could have been a destructive force and utilized it instead to inflate the bright bag that would eventually lift our craft. Without extreme heat, the aerial adventure would have remained grounded. Heat and pressure are necessary, whether creating a diamond or a Super Ball. Life sometimes brings the heat. When it does, you don't have to resign yourself to getting burned. Instead, you can harness the heat to elevate yourself and rise above the circumstances. Heat, when captured correctly, creates lift.

Another observation that I made was that while it's necessary to chart your course, you cannot always choose where you will finally land. Though we had a flight plan, our drop zone was ultimately determined by additional considerations. Wind speed and direction and finding a clearing safe enough to set down were factors that demanded our flexibility.

It's rarely ever a straight path to your goals.
While hope has a plan, it pursues that plan with an
understanding that there will be obstacles.

Life is a journey, with turns and detours in the road along the way. It's rarely ever a straight path to your goals. While hope has a plan, it pursues that plan with an understanding that there will be obstacles which may require choosing an alternate pathway, or even re-goaling at times. To be successful in any endeavor, you must set a course and take personal responsibility for your actions along the way. To a great extent, your choices will determine your destiny. But where you ultimately land will likely be influenced by conditions beyond your control. Wind currents and weather conditions are always changing. They may alter your flight. That's alright. There's joy in the journey.

It was also interesting to note that the winds that we experienced on the ground were hardly detectible once we were in the air. Rather than standing against them, we were being transported by them. There are times that we must brace ourselves against gale-force winds to stand firm and not lose our footing when it is necessary not to give ground. However, there are many times that it would be wiser to go with the flow rather than fight the inevitable. While fight or flight responses quickly deplete energy, learning to flow with the circumstances can conserve resources.

I am not suggesting that you allow yourself to be pushed around indiscriminately by the winds of chance nor drift away from your purpose. But, when expedient, momentum may be garnered by leveraging the wind, while controlling other elements of your flight. Sometimes it's just better to go with the flow and make adjustments along the way. Ride the wind and the waves when you can, while staying at the helm to navigate as necessary. Wisdom demands flexibility. Agility is the ability to take advantage of the wind currents and weather conditions. When riding with the wind, life is peaceful and carries you with minimal effort. Whenever possible, harness the power of the wind.

And lastly, if you are able to rise above the constraining circumstances of an earthbound existence, then your sightline significantly changes. When floating high above life's landscape, you can see things more clearly. Your field of vision increases. The horizon expands as you rise. An elevated perspective can change the way you see everything.

Life Cycles

World War I leveled economies the world over as it brought unprecedented death and destruction. In the United States, however, the situation was different. In fact, between 1914 and 1918, the U.S. mostly boomed as the government poured money into the wartime economy. In the midst of rampant inflation, the U.S. rose to be a global leader. Previously a debtor nation, America emerged from the war a chief lender with one of the strongest and most vibrant economies in the world. But just as life was stabilizing, it shifted again.

Many economists predicted a post-war crash as military factory orders dried up after the 1918 Armistice. Compounding the end of the wartime economy, a virulent contagion created a global pandemic. The Spanish Flu cut a deadly swath across nations worldwide, infecting a third of the planet's population and killing twenty million. From the fall of 1918 to late spring of 1919, the contagion killed over 675,000 Americans. Businesses were shuttered across the country as people were sequestered to quell the outbreak. On the heels of the pandemic, a depression gutted the economy in 1920 and 1921. It was a combination of punches that some predicted would lead to a knockout blow for the U. S. economy. It was a difficult time, but the dire post-war economic predictions didn't come true. At least not immediately.

America bounced back. Instead of faltering, the twenties came roaring back as the United States entered into a decade of unprecedented growth and prosperity. Consumers, who had patriotically scrimped and saved during wartime, began to live it up. Inflation ticked upward, along with prices. But consumers were willing to pay anything for a taste of freedom. Instead of the deflationary slump that had been widely anticipated, the economy experienced an inflationary boomlet. The inevitable did happen, but not on schedule. The depression would have to wait.

The Roaring Twenties earned its name, as the U.S. economy grew by 42 percent from 1921 to 1929. Historians argue that the factors that made the decade so profitable were less of an anomaly as it was a deep desire on the part of the American people to return to normalcy. The biggest technological advances of the 1920's were in development before World War I hit the "pause" button. The electrification of homes and factories, the introduction of household appliances, rapid adoption of the automobile, the development of commercial aircraft and the growth of commercial radio stations and cinemas were all a part of an economy on fire. America returned to normal economic growth and a normal business cycle.[70]

For a decade the U.S. economy flourished. Skyrocketing wealth was fueled largely by easy credit and stock market speculation. Eventually the piper would want his payment. But for a number of years people exhaled with a sigh of relief and celebrated. Between 1920 and 1929, the nation's wealth more than doubled and economic growth swept America into an affluent but unfamiliar consumer society. With extra money to spend, Americans purchased goods such as ready-to-wear clothes, home appliances and radios. By the end of the decade there were radios in more than twelve million homes. And people went to the movies. Historians estimate that, by the end of the decade, three-quarters of the population visited a movie theater every week. Americans loved to be entertained.

Phonograph records, which had become popularized by radio stations, were sold by the hundreds of millions. Jazz music swept the country. Cars afforded young people freedom and dancing became the American pastime. While prohibition curtailed some freedoms, the reality is that it simply drove the sale and consumption of liquor underground. Americans would not be denied their party.

I realize that history lessons may do little to assuage fears when someone is trying to stare down a potential catastrophe. But it still serves us well to remember that even the toughest of circumstances will eventually pass. The point is that history and life move in cycles. While a pandemic has the capacity to put the planet on pause, the earth will continue to spin on its axis. Life goes on. Economies rebound. And people are resourceful. The future is bright for those who have hope, no matter how dark the night they may now be experiencing. A new day will dawn. The sun will rise again. Gray clouds will eventually part and the winds will settle from the storm. Hold on. Embrace hope and grow. Anticipate and prepare to build a brighter tomorrow. Get ready for your comeback!

Your Setback May Be the Setup for Your Comeback

Giancarlo Cruz Michael Stanton is an outfielder and designated hitter for the New York Yankees. He made his Major League Baseball debut in 2010 as a member of the Miami Marlins, with whom he played until the end of the 2017 season. Stanton has twice led the National League in home runs. Known for his prodigious physical strength and ability to hit long home runs, he is one of the most valuable players in the league.

On June 6, 2010, the Marlins announced that Stanton would be called up to the MLB, making him the third youngest player in its history at the age of 20. It didn't take Stanton long to prove himself. After a stellar rookie season, he went on in his second season to amass a total of 56 career home runs before his 22nd birthday. The amazing feat matched Alex Rodriquez and lagged only Ken Griffey Jr. among players in the past 40 years.

But, on September 11, 2014, life pushed the pause button and his entire career became questionable. Facing pitcher Mike Fiers of the Milwaukee Brewers, Stanton stood in the batter's box, poised to hit another long ball. Fiers, known for his fastball, knew well the threat at the plate and decided to brush him back with a pitch high and inside. Unleashing the furry, he hurtled the solid, white orb toward the plate at blinding speed. Rather than flinch, Stanton stared down the blazing ball a little too long. The errant pitch struck Stanton squarely on the left cheek, knocking him to the ground and sending his manager and teammates scrambling to his side as the stands fell silent.

Carried from the diamond, Stanton had sustained multiple facial fractures, lacerations and dental damage. Less than a week later, the Marlins announced that he would not play the rest of the season. After suffering such a traumatic experience, many commentators questioned his ability to return to the game at the same high level of play. After all, how could someone step back in the batter's box after sustaining a fastball to the face and take another Major League pitch without their will wilting? Many wondered – but not Stanton. He had fought through injuries before and he wasn't about to flinch in the face of adversity. He never lost hope that he would be able to mount a comeback.

And come back he did – with a vengeance. For him, the bend in the road was not the end of the road. He came back swinging. And in 2017, Stanton led the major leagues in home runs (59), runs batted in (132), and slugging percentage (.631), winning the National League Most Valuable Player Award. For Giancarlo Stanton, the setback was merely a setup for his comeback.[71]

What do you do when life hits you in the face and knocks you to the ground? Many would understand if you never suited up again to take the field. After all, it can be unnerving to stand in the batter's box and take the heat once you've been struck solidly by challenging circumstances. But it's in times like these that hope becomes most valuable.

Hope reminds you that a bend in the road is not the end of the road. Hope renews the spirit. It creates the resilience to bounce back when you're thrown down.

Hope can give you the plan to prepare for your comeback. Hope allows you to get a vision for life on the other side of your injuries. Hope provides you with the will to work hard to rehab your dreams. Hope reminds you that a bend in the road is not the end of the road. Hope renews the spirit. It creates the resilience to bounce back when you're thrown down. And hope gives you the courage to stand in the batter's box again and swing for the fence.

Hope Rises

Our hot air balloon ride through the valleys of Napa will remain one of my favorite inflight experiences. It was an adventure that will be marked in my memory. Multi-colored balloons scattered across a cloudless sky is a beautiful sight to behold. The lessons I learned that day have forever marked me for the good. And they have shown me the power of hope to elevate life, love and leadership.

Hope begins when you choose to strategically harness the heat that life brings your way. Suffering, tough circumstances and setbacks are a part of life. Nobody is immune to chaos and calamity. Life happens. You can't control it. But you can control how you respond to adversity. You may not be able to control what happens around you, but you can certainly control what happens in you. Turn the burners inward and capture the energy to inflate your dreams again. Remember that no matter how hot the fiery trials that may come your way, hope makes your happiness fireproof.

Even if temporarily grounded, hope always has a flight plan. Before liftoff, hope takes into consideration wind currents and weather conditions and charts a course to a desired destination. Hope makes plans for an inspirational and exhilarating adventure. It's important to set goals that engender enthusiasm if you want the journey to be enjoyable.

Hope untethers you from the constraining circumstances of an earthbound existence. It allows you to rise above the chatter and the clamor of the crowd and brings a clarity that comes from a higher perspective.

Hope breaks the bonds that restrain you and prevent you from soaring to greater heights. It allows you to rise above the chatter and the clamor of the crowd and brings a clarity that comes from a higher perspective. It sets you free to act responsibly, taking full ownership of those elements that you can control. While there may be many factors beyond your control, hope focuses on what influence you can have and produces a confident assurance that your effort and energy will make a significant difference in the outcome. You aren't a victim. You have a say in how your life unfolds. The choices that you make and the actions that you take will determine your destiny. So, choose wisely and act responsibly.

And be flexible. The wind currents and weather conditions may likely change. And the landscape will factor into your final landing location. Agility means being prepared to adapt and be creative in adjusting the path you choose in reaching your goal. And, when circumstances dictate, be ready to re-goal. Sometimes you have to let go of your expectations and live wholeheartedly in the experience. When you do that, your struggles don't define you – you define your struggles. You can bring meaning to suffering and setbacks that can forever enhance your legacy.

Know that you will encounter obstacles. You will experience hardships, setbacks and loss. It's part of the package. But when you do, remember this: The depth of your grief is inversely proportionate to the height of your joy. This is true whether it relates to the death of a loved one or the death of a dream. The greater the love, the greater the loss. You can't have one without the other. That's life. That's the deal.

A well-lived life is not without losses or challenges. A well-lived life flows from a solid core of values and is created by good choices and responsible living. It does not avoid grief and loss. Rather it seeks and celebrates deeper love and greater joy. In other words, a life worth living finds its foundation in hope. And a life worth living fully embraces faith, hope and love.

Hope is by far the best strategy to build a life of meaning and purpose. Hope anchors life in the midst of the storms. Hope shapes the future. Hope instills courage. Hope elevates your perspective. Hope changes the way you view life. Hope helps you love deeper. Hope helps you lead more inspirationally. Hope provides the passion to pursue your dreams. Hope gives you the agility to adjust. Hope provides you with a plan to build a brighter tomorrow. Hope fills the soul and elevates the spirit. Life takes flight when hope rises.

Hope provides you with the means to harness the heat that life brings your way. Hope settles the soul and equips you to effectively extinguish anxiety. Hope affords you the possibility of enjoying a healthier, longer and more productive life. In short, hope is the essential element that makes life and happiness fireproof.

Part Three Challenge

GO TO: **FIREPROOFHAPPINESS.COM**

REGISTER FOR THE
FIREPROOF HAPPINESS DIGITAL COURSE

ENTER CODE: FH20 FOR A 20% DISCOUNT

Endnotes

1   Snyder, C. R., C. Harris, J. R. Anderson, S. A. Holleran, L. M. Irving, S. T. Sigmon, et al. "The Will and the Ways: Development and Validation of an Individual-Differences Measure of Hope," *Journal of Personality and Social Psychology*, 60 (1991): 570-585. pmid: 2037968

2   Snyder, C. R. "Hope Theory: Rainbows in the Mind." *Psychological Inquiry*, 13, no. 4 (2002): 249-275.

3   Snyder, C. R., K. L. Rand, and D. R. Sigmon. "Hope theory." In *Handbook of Positive Psychology*, 257-276. Oxford, England: Oxford University Press, 2002.

4   *Journal of Positive Psychology*, 2009

5   "Dixon, W. A., P. P. Heppner, and M. D. Rudd. Problem-Solving Appraisal, Hopelessness, and Suicide Ideation: Evidence for a Mediatorial Model. *Journal of Counseling Psychology*, 41 (1994): 91-98."

6   Beck, A. T., R. A. Steer, J. S. Beck, and C. F. Newman. "Hopelessness, Depression, Suicidal Ideation, and Clinical Diagnosis of Depression." *Suicide and Life-Threatening Behavior*, 23 (1993): 139-145. pmid: 8342213

7   Johnson, J., A. M. Wood, P. Gooding, P. J. Taylor, and N. Tarrier. "Resilience to Suicidality: The Buffering Hypothesis." *Clinical Psychology Review*, 31 (2011): 563-591. Pmid: 21276646

8   Duckworth A. L., C. Peterson, M. D. Mathews, and D. R. Kelly. "Grit: Perseverance and Passion for Long-Term Goals.: *Journal of Personality and Social Psychology*, 92 (2007): 1087-1101. pmid: 17547490

9   Kleiman, E. M., L. M. Adams, T. B. Kashdan, and J. H. Riskind. "Gratitude and Grit Indirectly Reduce Risk of Suicidal Ideations by Enhancing Meaning in Life: Evidence for a Mediated Moderation Model." *Journal of Research in Personality*, 47 (2013): 539-546.

10   Ibid, p. 545-546.

11   Seligman, Martin E. *Learned Optimism: How to Change Your Mind and Your Life*. New York, NY: Vintage Books, 2006, 14-16.

12   Snyder, C. R., and J. D. Taylor. "Hope as a Common Factor across Psychotherapy Approaches: A Lesson from the Dodo's Verdict." In *Handbook of Hope: Theory, Measures, and Applications*, edited by C. R. Snyder, 89-108. San Diego, CA: Academic Press, 2000.

13   Snyder, C. R. "Hypothesis: There is Hope." In *Handbook of Hope: Theory, Measures, and Applications*, edited by C. R. Snyder, 3-21. San Diego, CA: Academic Press, 2000.

14   Snyder, C. R., C. Harris, J. R. Anderson, S. A. Holleran, L. M. Irving, S. T. Sigmon, et al. "The Will and the Ways: Development and Validation of an Individual-Differences Measure of Hope," *Journal of Personality and Social Psychology*, 60 (1991): 571. pmid: 2037968

15   Beck, A. T., A. Weissman, D. Lester, and L. Trexler. "The Measurement of Pessimism: The Hopelessness Scale." *Journal of Consulting and Clinical Psychology*, 42 (1974): 861-865. pmid: 4436473

16   Brown, G. K., A. T. Beck, R. A. Steer, and J. R. Grisham. "Risk Factors for Suicide in Psychiatric Outpatients: A 20-Year Prospective Study." *Journal of Consulting and Clinical Psychology*, 68 2000: 371-377. pmid: 10883553

17   Huen, J. M. Y., B. Y. T. lp, S. M. Y. Ho, and P. S. F. Yip "Hope and Hopelessness: The Role of Hope in Buffering the Impact of Hopelessness on Suicidal Ideation." *PLoS ONE* 10 (2015), no. 6: e0130073. https://doi.org/10.1371/journal.pone.0130073

18   "About Travis Mills," Travis Mills Group, accessed on May 12, 2020. https://www.travismills.org/about/.

19   Lawson, D. *Posterity: Letters of Great Americans to Their Children*. New York, NY: Broadway Books, 2004, 96-97.

20   Ibid, p. 97.

21   *Life Magazine*, May 14, 1965, 93-122.

22   James H. Duff. *An American Vision: Three Generations of Wyeth Art*, Boston, MA: Little Brown & Company, 1987, p. 123

23   Cross, Rod. "Measurements of the Horizontal Coefficient of Restitution for a Superball and a Tennis Ball." *American Journal of Physics*, 70 (May 2002), no. 5:482-489.

24   Stronge, W. J. *Impact Mechanics*. Cambridge, UK: Cambridge University Press, 2004, 112.

25 Wulffson, Don L., and Laurie Keller. *Toys! Amazing Stories Behind Some Great Inventions*. New York, NY: Henry Holt and Co., 2000, 92-94.

26 MacCambridge, Michael. *America's Game*. New York, NY: Random House, 2004, 237.

27 Avey, J. B., J. L. Patera, and B. J. West, "The Implications of Positive Psychological Capital on Employee Absenteeism," *Journal of Leadership and Organizational Studies* 13 (2006): 42-60.

28 Peterson, S. J., and K. Byron, "Exploring the Role of Hope in Job Performance: Results from Four Studies," *Journal of Organizational Behavior* 29 (2008): 785-803.

29 Ibid., 785-803.

30 Peterson, S. J., F. O. Walumbwa, K. Byron, and J. Myrowitz, "CEO Positive Psychological Traits, Transformational Leadership, and Firm Performance in High-Technology Start-Up and Established Firms," *Journal of Management* 35 (2008), no.2: 348-68.

31 Lopez, Shane J. *Making Hope Happen: Creating the Future You Want for Yourself and Others*. New York, NY: Atria Books, 2013, 54-55.

32 Ibid., 50-55.

33 Ibid., 50-55.

34 Diener, E., "Subjective Well-Being," *Psychological Bulletin* 95 (1984): 542-75.

35 Gallagher, M. W., and S. J. Lopez, "Positive Expectancies and Mental Health: Identifying the Unique Contributions of Hope and Optimism," *Journal of Positive Psychology* 4 (1984): 542-75.

36 Achtziger, A., P. M. Gollwitzer, and P. Sheeran, "Implementation Intentions and Shielding Goal Striving from Unwanted Thoughts and Feelings," *Personality and Social Psychology Bulletin* 34 (2008): 381-93.

37 Feldman, D. B., and C. R. Snyder, "Hope and the Meaningful Life: Empirical and Theoretical Associations between Goal-Directed Thinking and Life Meaning," *Journal of Social and Clinical Psychology* 24 (2005): 401-21.

38 Snyder, C. R., S. J. Lopez, and J. T. Pedrotti, *Positive Psychology: The Scientific and Practical Explorations of Human Strengths*. Thousand Oaks, CA: Sage, 2010.

39 Lopez, Shane J. *Making Hope Happen: Creating the Future You Want for Yourself and Others*. New York, NY: Atria Books, 2013, 57-59.

40 Stern, S., R. Dhanda, and H. Hazuda, "Hopelessness Predicts Mortality in Older Mexican and European Americans," *Psychosomatic Medicine* 63 (2001): 344-51.

41 Lopez, Shane J. New York, NY: Atria Books, 2013, 61.

42 Collins, Jim. *Good to Great*. New York, NY: Harper Business, 2001, 83-85.

43 Nuwer, Rachel. "There Are Over 200 Bodies on Mount Everest, and They're Used as Landmarks," *Smithsonian Magazine*, November 28, 2012, https://www.smithsonianmag.com/smart-news/there-are-over-200-bodies-on-mount-everest-and-theyre-used-as-landmarks-146904416/.

44 "Matematik-professoren leger med lego-klodser," Roshanzamir, Ali. Accessed on March 29, 2014. https://www.science.ku.dk/presse/nyhedsarkiv/2013/leger-med-lego-klodser/.

45 Robinson, Sarita. "What are the effects of total isolation? An expert explains," *The Conversation*, January 4, 2019, https://theconversation.com/what-are-the-effects-of-total-isolation-an-expert-explains-109091#.

46 Diamond, Stephen A. "Let's Talk About Loneliness: Alienation in a Linked Up Age," *Psychology Today* (blog), February, 21, 2014, https://www.psychologytoday.com/us/blog/evil-deeds/201402/lets-talk-about-loneliness-alienation-in-linked-age.

47 Grossman, Stan. "Social Support Could Increase BDNF levels, Decreasing Risk of Stroke and Dementia," *Neurology Advisor*, April 16, 2016, https://www.neurologyadvisor.com/conference-highlights/aan-2016-coverage/social-support-could-increase-bdnf-levels-decrease-risk-for-stroke-and-dementia/.

48 Castrodale, Jelisa. "The World's Last Blockbuster Remains Open, Pandemic and Netflix Be Damned," Vice, May 12, 2020, https://www.vice.com/en_us/article/n7wwnq/the-worlds-last-blockbuster-remains-open-pandemic-and-netflix-be-damned.

49 Ibid.

50 Gladwell, Malcom. *Blink: The Power of Thinking Without Thinking*. New York, NY: Back Bay Books, 2005.

51 Hughes, Stuart "The Greatest Motivational Poster Ever?", *BBC News*, February 4, 2009, http://news.bbc.co.uk/1/hi/magazine/7869458.stm.

52 Lewis, Rebecca. "Keep Calm and Carry on and other Second War Posters: British Home Front Propaganda Posters of the Second World War," April 5, 2009, http://ww2poster.co.uk/2009/02/1939-3-posters/

53 Frankl, Viktor. *Man's Search for Meaning*. Boston, MA: Beacon Press, 2006, 71-77.

54 Frankl, Viktor. *The Doctor and the Soul: From Psychotherapy to Logotherapy*. New York, NY: Vintage Books, 1986, 162.

55   Shapiro, Fred R. "Who Wrote the Serenity Prayer?", The Chronicle of Higher Education, April 28, 2014, https://www.chronicle.com/article/Who-Wrote-the-Serenity-Prayer-/146159.

56   Frankl, Viktor. *Man's Search for Meaning*. Revised edition. New York, NY: Washington Square Press, 1985, 58.

57   Gould, W. B., and Viktor E. Frankl: *Life with Meaning*. Pacific Grove, CA: Brooks/Cole Publishing. 1993, 47.

58   Frankl, Viktor. p. 97.

59   Ibid., 165.

60   Frankl, Viktor. *The Doctor and the Soul: From Psychotherapy to Logotherapy*. New York, NY: Vintage Books, 1986, 33.

61   Tillich, Paul. *The Dynamics of Faith*. New York, NY: Harper Collins, 1958, 220.

62   Maddi, S. "Hardiness: An Operationalization of Existential Courage." *Journal of Humanistic Psychology*, 44 (2004): 279-298.

63   Chu, Henry. "Keep Calm and Carry on ... into a Feud." *The Sydney Morning Herald*. May 4, 2013, http://www.smh.com.au/world/keep-calm-and-carry-on-into-a-feud-20130503-2ix55.html.

64   Jordan, Anthony J. *Christy Brown's Women: A Biography Drawing on His Letters*. Westport, CT: Westport Books, 1998.

65   Brown, Brené. *Daring Greatly: How the Courage to Be Vulnerable Transforms the Way We Live, Love, Parent, and Lead*. New York, NY: Avery, 2012.

66   Frankl, Viktor. *Man's Search for Meaning*. Boston, MA: Beacon Press, 2006, xiv-xv.

67   Lucas, Jim. "Newton's Laws of Motion." *LiveScience*, September 27, 2017, https://www.livescience.com/46558-laws-of-motion.html.

68   Frankl, Viktor. *Man's Search for Meaning*. Boston, MA: Beacon Press, 2006, 65-66.

69   Hambleton, Georgina L. *Christy Brown: The Life That Inspired My Left Foot*. Edinburgh, United Kingdom: Mainstream Publishing, 2007, 240.

70   Roos, Dave. "When WWI, Pandemic and Slump Ended, Americans Sprung into the Roaring Twenties." April 24, 2020. https://www.history.com/news/pandemic-world-war-i-roaring-twenties.

71   "Giancarlo Stanton," Wikipedia, Wikimedia Foundation, last modified June 23, 2020, at 04:00, https://en.wikipedia.org/wiki/Giancarlo_Stanton.

Acknowledgments

Life is made rich by those with whom we choose to share it. By that standard, I am truly a rich man. I have been the recipient of the love and grace demonstrated by a whole host of folks. While it would not be possible for me to list all of the people who have profoundly influenced my life and writing, I would like to take a moment and thank a few of them:

To my wife, LuAnne, and our children, Ryan, Lindsay, Colton and Jonathan: We make a good team. Challenging times have refined us all as we have dealt with the frailties of one another. But love and hope will forever mark our lives and our future. May we continue to grow together to experience the richness of life, grow in our love and make many more wonderful memories together.

To my agent, Chris Ferebee: I want to express my deep gratitude for your friendship, support and encouragement on each project. We are getting better together. Thanks for being in my corner.

To my branding guru, Jayson Teagle, and the Collideoscope World team: Without a nudge from you, this project would have most likely stayed on the shelf. Thank you for prodding me to get this message into the market in a timely fashion. May it have the impact that we both believe it can have.

To my editor, Michelle Rapkin: It is always so refreshing to banter ideas back and forth with you. Your encouragement in the content and your corrections of my grammar have produced a message that can make a difference. Thank you for being a cheerleader and friend.

To Kay Acton, my sister-in-law and editor extraordinaire, who fine-tuned the language and grammar to make the content flow and the message more effective. You are one in a million and I am grateful for your advice and encouragement.

To Rob Kosberg and the Best Seller Publishing team: Thank you for your time, energy and dedication to getting this message into the market in such a timely fashion and helping me garner the attention of the masses.

To my good friends, Charles Buffington, Kay Acton, Susan Clark and Scott MacLellan: I am truly grateful to have folks like you in my life who would invest their time in wading through the rough draft of this work and offering your feedback. You have made this a better work through your suggestions.

To my friends and clients: Without your support, none of this would be possible. Thank you for allowing me the privilege to invest in your teams. May the principles and practices that I espouse continue to have a profound impact on your life and leadership, as we build a brighter tomorrow together.

Dr. Randy Ross

D r. Randy Ross is a compelling communicator, craftsman of culture and bestselling author of multiple books, including *Remarkable! Maximizing Results Through Value Creation, The Roadmap to Remarkable!,* and *Relationomics: Business Powered by Relationships.*

Working with brands like GE Appliances, Cox Communications, Compass Group, Chick-fil-A, Keller Williams and the Intercontinental Hotel Group, he has inspired and enabled countless people to find new passion and purpose in their work, work better together in teams and have greater influence and impact.

When people like what they do, they do it better. When people like those they do it with, they work better together. When they like the impact they are having, they find meaning and fulfillment in what they do. Dr. Ross helps them find what they really like, while building healthier relationships and pursuing a passion beyond self.

As the CEO of Remarkable and a former Chief People Officer, Dr. Randy Ross utilizes his experience to engage audiences worldwide with his keen insight and contagious humor. He is a messenger of practical wisdom and needed hope, untangling the biggest challenges facing today's business leader, tomorrow's workforce and the future marketplace. He lives with his wife, LuAnne, and four children in Atlanta, Georgia.

CONNECT WITH

Dr. Randy Ross

FOR ADDITIONAL RESOURCES, VISIT:
WWW.FIREPROOFHAPPINESS.COM

FOR SPEAKING ENGAGEMENTS, VISIT:
WWW.DRRANDYROSS.COM

Made in the USA
Columbia, SC
09 October 2023